LETTER TO A FUTURE LOVER

LETTER TO A FUTURE LOVER

Marginalia, Errata, Secrets, Inscriptions, and
Other Ephemera Found in Libraries

ANDER MONSON

Graywolf Press

This publication is made possible, in part, by the voters of Minnesota through a Minnesota State Arts Board Operating Support grant, thanks to a legislative appropriation from the arts and cultural heritage fund, and through a grant from the Wells Fargo Foundation Minnesota. Significant support has also been provided by Target, the McKnight Foundation, Amazon.com, and other generous contributions from foundations, corporations, and individuals. To these organizations and individuals we offer our heartfelt thanks.

Published by Graywolf Press
250 Third Avenue North, Suite 600
Minneapolis, Minnesota 55401

All rights reserved.

www.graywolfpress.org

Published in the United States of America
Printed in Canada

ISBN 978-1-55597-706-1

2 4 6 8 9 7 5 3 1
First Graywolf Printing, 2015

Library of Congress Control Number: 2014948534

Cover design and art: Marian Bantjes

This book is for Megan and Athena,

the first two entries on the first shelf.

LETTER TO A FUTURE LOVER

Date Due		
FEB 17 '47		
Sluff		

is an arbitrary place to start, I know, my hand inside a book, my heart inside a book, this one Pierce Butler's *Books and Libraries in Wartime* (1945), not checked out since its last returning sixty-eight years ago. To run a finger along this page is to consult a reading record and to caress the past. I address the past with this list of lovelinesses, things I found in libraries over years. Years are threats that libraries oppose, even if eventually it's necessary to weed the stacks: we can't keep everything forever.

Sixty-eight years without a reader! More than the duration of a life for many (especially during war), still it isn't so much, reader, in geologic time. (What is a moraine but a tectonic collection?) Yet still it speaks. What do libraries mean in wartime? What do they mean when we are not at war? We are currently at war, even if it's easy to forget our foreign complications unless someone we love is over there. The names of those beloved and how they felt and smelled to us become a constant hum that soundtracks our days until they are returned on a designated date, also like a book. A book is taken out. Perhaps it is read. Then it is returned. Or in some cases it just rests on a reader's bookshelf unremembered. Or maybe the last patron died of dehydration with this book in hand and it was placed aside respectfully when she was found, and it was cleaned and deemed relevant enough to return it these decades later, so only a week ago it made it back, thus explaining the long lapse in our attentions to its contents. Instead it was loved and read each night, maybe because it documented a tiny story, say that of the makeshift Vilna ghetto library under German occupation, one that might otherwise be forgotten beneath all the other stories if the patron did not reread it each night. To archive is political. To keep a story on a shelf or to remember then retell it means that it will be more likely to exist to those who come after we have gone. It will all be gone in time. Maybe this is the best we can do.

In this place of preservation, it's not hard to be reminded of those we've lost or fear we might, those who were due but never came. A librarian's conversation, a spine-cracked paperback, a human hair, a whiff of sandalwood in air: each of these might disappear for a year or more and fold the past into the present and pound a nail through the intersection. Patron, in this way we're young again; we remember; we're alive.

Might as well be the start of something artful, an entry point or an attempt to open. I don't just mean the poet Ai though you could try her too, from beyond or from a book, where what is left of her now resides after she passed. Maybe I mean the maned sloth, found only on the eastern edge of Brazil, which takes its name from sin and is ill-branded for the future. It's on a slow boat there with its tufts of fur and its disdain for our accelerated lives. These sloths "rarely descend from the trees because, when on a level surface, they are unable to stand and walk, only being able to drag themselves along with their front legs and claws. They travel to the ground only to defecate or to move between trees when they cannot do so through the branches. The sloth's main defenses are to stay still and to lash out with its formidable claws." I quote from Wikipedia because, like the ai, I prefer to stay still and lash out with my formidable claws. Oh, that is obviously a lie. I have claws but will not stay still for long. By trying to I hope to learn something new. The ai's habitat is constantly under threat.

Maybe you already know that a book is an artificial intelligence, designed to be tried on and played obsessively like a software subroutine, a difficult first-person shooter scene, or a favorite song you've listened to too long. You're here because you liked its eyes, the way it dots them with hearts in handwritten notes from years ago. Try it on for size. Ideally you found this AI in a library, its natural habitat, an ideal vehicle for speaking to the future, even if it is under threat. But everything is threatened in this age. It's as if nothing can shine or mean unless we threaten it with axes, with budget cuts, with obsolescence, with oblivion.

You should know this is not the only version of the book. First, it snuck in under others' covers, a little at a time. I sent these essays into the world inside books I found and spent an hour or more inside. Some of these were subsequently re-printed, bound or loose, in magazines. Then it was in a box, unordered, unbound, big and pretty and fancy in a limited edition. I liked that fine.

Here you'll find it too, the book, the book about the book, and those who give over our homes and lives to books and share their habitats. These are only in an order because binding makes it so: alphabetical is arbitrary. It also leaves an odor. Read the entries in whichever way you like. Be slothful and go straight through, claws extended, or stay still and hope the world will come to you. I'd start with

"How to Read a Book," myself, if I didn't already know how to navigate these things. Use it as you would any of its class. Adjust it like a sextant. Let it open up a seam in you like Anne Sexton. Discard—or not—when finished, like a former lover's breath, like a pdf.

Special Librarie:

Official Journal of the Special Libraries Association

April 1940

AN ALPHABET

IS AN APHRODISIAC

★ PARTIAL LIST OF ORGANIZATIONS IN WHICH SPECIAL LIBRARIES ARE OPERATING ★

ADVERTISING AGENCIES   AERONAUTICAL MANUFACTURERS   AGRICULTURAL COLLEGES   ARCHITE
OFFICES   ART MUSEUMS   AUTOMOBILE MANUFACTURERS   BAKING COMPANIES   BANKS   BOTA
GARDENS   BROADCASTING SYSTEMS   CAMERA CLUBS   CEMENT MANUFACTURERS   CHAIN STO
CHAMBERS OF COMMERCE   CHARITY ORGANIZATIONS   CHEMICAL COMPANIES   CHURCHES   CL
CONSUMER RESEARCH AGENCIES   DAIRY LEAGUES   DENTAL SCHOOLS   DEPARTMENT STO
ELECTRIC LIGHT COMPANIES   ELECTRICAL MANUFACTURERS   FOOD DISTRIBUTORS   FOREST SERV
FOUNDATIONS   FRATERNAL ORGANIZATIONS   FRUIT COMPANIES   FUND-RAISERS   GAS COMPAN
GLASS MANUFACTURERS   GROCERY CHAINS   HEALTH OFFICES   HISTORICAL SOCIETIES   HOSPIT
HOTELS   INDUSTRIAL ENGINEERS   INDUSTRIAL RESEARCH LABORATORIES   INSTRUMENT COMPAN
INSURANCE COMPANIES   INVESTMENT COUNSELORS   INVESTMENT TRUSTS   LABOR BURE
LAUNDRIES   LAW FIRMS   LUMBER DEALERS   MAIL ORDER HOUSES   MANAGEMENT ENGINE
MARKETING CONSULTANTS   MEDICAL ASSOCIATIONS   MERCHANDISERS   MICROFILM MANUFACTUR
MINING COMPANIES   MILK DISTRIBUTORS   MOTION PICTURE COMPANIES   MUNITIONS MANUFACTUR
MUSEUMS OF SCIENCE   MUSIC INSTITUTES   NEWSPAPERS   OFFICE EQUIPMENT MANUFACTUR
PAINT MANUFACTURERS   PAPER MANUFACTURERS   PATENT DEPARTMENTS   PETROLEUM REFINEI
PHARMACEUTICAL MANUFACTURERS   PLAYGROUNDS   PRINTERS   PRISONS   PUBLIC RELATI
COUNSELORS   PUBLIC ROADS BUREAUS   PUBLISHERS   REAL ESTATE BOARDS   REFRIGERA'
MANUFACTURERS   RELIEF ORGANIZATIONS   RESEARCH FOUNDATIONS   SAFETY ASSOCIATI

—*Special Libraries,* April 1940 (University of Arizona Library, Main)

for a certain sort of reader, isn't it? To know there is a list like this is to want to penetrate it deeply, to understand its depths and pockmarked passages, to need to see where they lead eventually. So what if I know I cannot get to all of them? To know that they are sorted there, that they are there for me if I choose to follow is perhaps enough. But surely some have gone extinct, are sacrosanct, private, inaccessible, classified, destroyed, closed, hidden, erased, or otherwise beyond my means.

Knowing an infinity is there and unknowable (for that is what an infinity is, unknowable, unfathomable, though we try to hold it in the word *infinity,* we know that wall won't hold it long) is sublime; it lets a bit of air into the mind. Still it's a lovely list, a laundry list of possibilities, of libraries buried in laundries, as it suggests. If you've been to one in search of cleaning you may have noticed they contain magazines on tables or in a crate, perhaps the occasional book. Read, deposit one, or take one home. It's a song that plays whether you partake or do not. Likewise those embedded in hotels and B&Bs, for instance the former Days Hotel in Grand Rapids, Michigan, where I like to stay when I'm in town, with its shelf of cheapo paperbacks, a trail of reading material left behind by those who came before, wherein I find a way to pass an hour that doesn't involve the *Law & Order* television blare.

I venerate you for your generosity, former patron, even if you did not mean to lend or leave this book and thought that you packed or discarded it or just forgot. I venerate you too, who cleaned the rooms and gathered books for the collection. These are here for our protection. With too much time alone who knows what compartment of ourselves we might discover? Better to fill it with another's words. I venerate the gods of randomness whose altars these collections are. Maybe it's enough to take a book and read a couple of pages and give it back. Or perhaps you will take a title home. Perhaps you've discarded it when you were done and what I find is not evidence of a randomly selected group but one woman's leavings, her trail of readings.

Over coffee one afternoon in the summer of 2001, András reminded me of another way to burn books, explained to him by a colleague who survived the siege of Sarajevo. In the winter, the scholar and his wife ran out of firewood, and so began to burn their books for heat and cooking. "This forces one to think critically," András remembered his friend saying. "One must prioritize. First, you burn old college textbooks, which you haven't read in thirty years. Then there are the duplicates. But eventually, you're forced to make tougher choices. Who burns today: Dostoevsky or Proust?"

—Matthew Battles, *Library: An Unquiet History*

If you are in duress, burn this first. I give you my permission. My position is that this is disposable, like electronic text, like ticker tape, track for news of stocks, the earliest digital electronic communications medium. The first invention Edison sold, his "Electrical Printing Instrument," was patented November 9, 1869. It was not the first stock printer, though Edison's remains the best known. 1867 saw E. A. Calahan's first machine. 1871 introduced the "Unison Device," which would "stop the type-wheels of all the printing-instruments in a circuit at a given point, so that they will all print alike when in operation"—which would bring all the tickers on a network into unison, so that information would synchronize and propagate. There's that moment in which what seemed like chaos is no longer, and things align, a structure's found. Impossible, perhaps, to overstate how significant this concept was: networked machines, distributing simultaneous information a century before the Internet.

So read this once then secret it away for the next to troll these pages: this is meant for obsolescence. Maybe these sentences are already obsolete. But in a pinch it can be burned. This is not a sacred text, unlike the Quran, the word of God, which "does not include instructions for its own disposal," and should be buried, erased, or stored indefinitely; alternately, "desanctify the book by removing the text from its pages. Some medieval scholars recommend wiping off the ink and disposing of the paper by ordinary means. A more modern and practical alternative is to tie the book to a stone, then drop it into a stream to symbolically achieve the same effect" (these quotes via Slate.com, and for all I know (the scholar sighs (these eddies within eddies)) the article might already have disappeared). Sacred Jewish texts should be placed into a repository to await mass burial. Though a Bible has no built-in disposal ritual, and thus it can be burned, one should generally avoid burning sacred books because of fire's association with the devil and the underworld.

While you can't hold on to everything forever, you're a fool if you sell back your college books at semester's end: have you learned nothing of this life? Reread that book you disliked in ninth grade and see how it sings to you now: you understand the story differently because your own has changed. To celebrate your growth, throw yourself a ticker tape parade for and of your disposed-of books—confettied by clouds of shredded pages, call yourself a nebula of assorted information. In bits they are much easier to burn, though the flame won't last as long.

Though we call it that, we haven't used ticker tape in ticker tape parades for years: now it's all confetti, shredded financial documents shotgunned out in clouds over Broadway as whoever passes now for heroes processes below. For the last ticker tape parade, 2012, celebrating the New York Giants' Super Bowl win, a half-ton of confetti was distributed in twenty-five-pound bags to the buildings all along its route.

What else we drop: calls, balls, 7 in handheld smartphone games, in certain cases walls, ceilings filled with secrets we stashed as adolescents above the chewy tile: all of these literally, even how we say "literally" now, meaning its opposite, *metaphorically,* trying to redirect our attention to the figure of speech, to refresh and amp it up.

I hope you are lucky enough not to have to burn your books for fire or food. Reading networks sentences, memes them, beams them between brains in surprising ways: what's kept, what's stuck there, what's lodged in a cul-de-sac after the rest has left. It's like a game, a labyrinth. Everything in time becomes a trivium—in the latter half of the twentieth century, "knowledge that is nice to have but not essential"—originally *trivium* referred to one of the three topics of basic education (grammar, logic, rhetoric), though now it's for those inclined to marginalia, cultural crud that cakes the brain, knowledge acquired at random, obsessively, used in games like Pursuit or in game shows, or to impress those you meet at parties, papering over your lack of actual classical learning like a defiant shot across the bow of those who tried to educate you. Your meanders in the shredded trenches of Wikipedia minutiae and rarely visited library stacks have to pay off eventually. They will, won't they? Please say they will. If we say these words out loud together, we will be as one, in unison, synchronized with this device, the page.

It's as if the books in the library are just books with nothing in them except more books.

—Lucy Corin, "Library,"
One Hundred Apocalypses and other Apocalypses

What I can't comprehend is endlessness. The lives of saints. The horrors they endured to be so deemed. How they gleam in our remaining light before the candle gutters and is extinguished and instead we have the dark. How items packed by weight, not volume, settle during shipping and become a tangled bundle. The spaces between things—books, call numbers, thoughts of love and death. How they're reconfigured by our constant jostling. In this way things settle and will gradually fuse. These jumbles of disconnect become our memories, solid as a rack. I mean a rock. I mean a brackish pond, a murk, how a solid-seeming thing becomes a wash. We soothe them over time, wear them down with use, make them smooth with all the ways we adjust to make them fit our narratives. Oh, *that's* what that loaded moment meant. That one awkward pause in a conversation that comes to mind a decade later: only now do we understand attraction, our predilections for misinterpretation and our own reactions to being adored and not noticing it for years: how the idea of starlight as history frightens us.

The more I visit libraries the more I find myself opening up to them. There are so many passages in these labyrinths that it's impossible to see them all or to note their passing. Better to settle for the few I can find my way to wend through for a year or two. Some libraries are dying. A few I've seen are filled with wind (no, not the Wind of Change, as the Scorpions remind, but an air-conditioned breeze that reminds us this place needs tending to, in order to remain in its condition). Others are contracting, transforming, weeding books, adding more security, offering more machines for our use, rebooting with coffee shops and apps or fishing poles (like the Honeoye Public Library) or libraries of people (as in the Human Library, which offers people on loan to converse with). Or idiosyncratic ones like the Little Free Library tucked with children's books just down your street. Another is established as a subset of a public library and curates books from the larger set. One pops up for a week in a vacation town. You can do this yourself if you are crafty and don't mind a little risk: take the books that mean the most to you and set them on an empty shelf. Now label it. Add a note about who you are and what you're here for if the books you choose do not reveal enough. Then leave it, hope it will become a home to someone searching for reminder that our intelligence is good for something besides depression.

Finally that is what we love: human taint, human constraint. Not infinity but the best a man can grasp. (Is it sad that the television echoes back *Gillette*?) What a woman makes of or takes away from all these years and words, what she writes, what she returns, what she retains. Every essay suggests a new direction I might wander in the next, another space to aggregate and think about, another chamber in which to spend my hours, a currency that becomes more apparent as I age. Each book in which you lose yourself equals ten thousand you will not have time to read. See how your time spent in front of screen replaces your time in front of page? I'm not judging. I love my Xbox too, my Xanax too, my Xerox too, my xeriscaping too. (I am hopeful that we are coming to the end of lawns: a colossal water waste, our hours of pointless grooming.)

Let these adventures grow in each of us. The labyrinths we wander through in games, in dungeon-exploration games, in first-person shooter games, in mobile phone geocaching games: how different are they from our experience in text? When we drop down into a sentence, first-person-like, how a needle POVs a record groove, and see only the walls of what's on either side, parallel lines of peripheral sentences, not immediately related but separated by punctuation or a half-apparent phrase—when we get so deep into its interior that nothing exists outside it, when we abandon ourselves to its syntactic turns, its lines of preserved thought: every day we should be so lost.

Wayne Walker, member of the Nashville Songwriters Hall of Fame, noted for such compositions as "Burning Memories," "Are You Sincere?," and "Cajun Queen," January 2, 1979

Floyd Franklin Reed, Missouri old-time fiddler, February 1, 1979

Rodney and Will Balfa, members of the Balfa Brothers, Cajun musicians, February 8, 1978

Charles Seeger, Dean of American ethnomusicologists, the father of Pete, Peggy, and Mike, February 7, 1979

—*Journal of Country Music* 8.3, 1981
(University of Arizona Fine Arts Library)

I can't write you in a book without talking about death, since each book is a little death, and good country is nothing if not mourning. Any writer will tell you this: that publication is a separation, train leaving the station. It might indeed return, but it will not be the same. There's a psychological term for this that I forget: how any bodily fluid, once it's left the body, becomes alien, other, repellent. For instance: spit in a cup. Now drink it back up. Few of us will. Why not? It was in your mouth a moment ago. Isn't it yours? Isn't it you? It's easy to see our flaws in others, as we know. Less easy—and often painful, so we resist it—to appraise the self.

A book trains us for our end: each attenuates, you can feel the weight of its diminishing pages as you flip, and there's that final turn; at last its last is in view with only blankness after, like reaching a coast. It's bittersweet at best, reader, when one you've loved for long ends like this. Of course the sentences continue in your memory: how lines from Arthur C. Clarke or Beverly Cleary return to mind a decade later or longer. How we channel what we read—how we are channeled by it. How reading is experience, which every reader knows (though recent studies have finally proved this fact), and when we are confronted with a library full of these possible lives, we are awed by how much we do not know about the world. We cannot contain even a fraction of this information. We step away to clear our heads. We're not dead, yet, not today.

Until its recent renovation, Kansas State University's main library stacks were not air-conditioned, and sported signs that warned people with heart conditions to enter at their own risk in summer. So we will read in the face of danger—and that we can contain what we do read, if only for a moment, before it is/we are released. That we die is what gives our being meaning. Going through a loved one's books after they have passed, we might find their mind alive again in marginalia.

Knowing we can't have everything: what kind of life is this? How can we continue to exist? Except we do. And then we're through, and hopefully someone will mourn your loss, or maybe not, I don't know what kind of life you've lived, how much you read, how well you read, or if you read, if you were read, or who you touched and for how long and how and when and why and what it meant. If you're lucky you might be listed in a place like this, back of the *Journal of Country Music*, chronologically by date of death, with why you mattered, briefly, summed up in a sentence. (I almost wrote *summer up*, but did not, and now I did and didn't, honoring my errors: consider the ways the brain might (mis-)direct our energies, switch tracks without us noticing; perhaps these are the hidden intentions of the sentence we are always working on until we stop and see where we ended up.) So: Warren Smith, "rockabilly innovator who switched to honky-tonk," Ralph Sloan, simply a "clog dancer," Cousin Emmy (Cynthia May Carver), "the quintessential 'banjo-pickin' gal,'" James Price, "veteran bus driver for Ernest Tubb and Bill Anderson," and this strange list goes on. I don't know their names until I do. Life too goes on. Some clichés are true. There's not much between me and you besides this sentence, a paper card, this intake of breath. We too go on until we don't. I know so little of this world.

What do you know? I wonder. Why did or do you matter? What have you left of yourself behind?

8. Somewhere after news of his death, after anger, she felt the need
   to be kind.

9. I think too much. I will go on this trip to an unfamiliar place
   to find Joseph and talk to him and live in the present.

—Steve Orlen, *Crime of Omission* (unpublished manuscript, personal archive)

Outside poet Steve Orlen's former office door, I found three garbage bags marked *for trash*. He had died four months or so before. I looked inside. They were filled with notes and manuscripts. Shouldn't there be an archive for this stuff? I had dinner plans that night so I couldn't dally long, but I triaged out what bits I could that felt too awful to discard. I kept a small box, returned the rest. It is hard to know what matters.

The novel's not that good, I'm sure he'd admit, which is probably why he never published it. A genre thing, or a couple of drafts of one, with a bunch of reader's notes, some in Orlen's hand. On one page I found a note, presumably his son's:

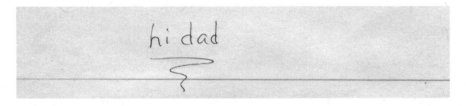

I felt this too should be preserved. Maybe that makes me sentimental. It's a shame we value product over process, though I suppose we must. A pentimento such as this might demonstrate a change from note to final draft. If we care enough about the work we might go deeper into the mine shaft of the draft, going farther down with the candles that we bought with our meager pay. But what if we discard those drafts and call them trash? We might believe the work we do is solo moan, and some long nights it is. Other times our progeny might scrawl notes so we know that they were there and participating silently. Or what our lover said to us last night in anger might shift a sentence's direction without our thinking of it.

In the era of nearly infinite data it remains easy to disappear. Now I'm housed in Orlen's former office. I have, in a case, a pack of Lucky Strikes that he kept from

1948. He smoked a lot; he died from it; it still smells a little like his smoke in here. Perhaps his smoke will continue rising up. I keep it as a shrine, another thing of his, just rolled leaves and paper that he never saw fit to burn.

I keep wondering: what have I left out that I should have said, that I could have kept? Our last conversation now feels freighted, as last conversations will. He was a conversation lover. Walking to the student union with him to enjoy caffeine, he asked me if there was ever a time when I stepped away from writing for a while, just gave it up and did something else, and if it was hard to make it back. I thought at the time it was kind of him to ask for my advice, as little as I had to give. He'd written longer and deeper than I could have dreamed. He said he was going to take some time away, but feared he wouldn't make it back. I don't remember what I said but wish I did. He never made it back.

Hot afternoons are real; afternoons are; places, things, thoughts, feelings are;
    poetry is;
The world is waiting to be known; Earth, what it has in it! The past is in it;
All words, feelings, movements, words, bodies, clothes, girls, trees, stones,
    things of beauty, books, desires are in it; and all are to be known;
Afternoons have to do with the whole world;

—Eli Siegel, *Hot Afternoons Have Been in Montana: Poems*
(PS3537 I295 H6 1957 mn)

There is no home for this brokenness, how neither the Dewey numbering nor the Library of Congress system is continuous, so you're always missing something, the perfect text, perhaps, between PS3537 I295 H6 1957 mn (above) and PS 3537 I317 T5 1939 (William Vincent Sieller's *This Transient Hour*). Spent an hour in contemplation, and while I know no library can be all-encompassing, and that it's all just alphabetical, the space between Siegel's breathless iterating lines and Sieller's sonnetteering is a world, as is the disconnect between Siegel's poems and the philosophy he founded (Aesthetic Realism, "the art of liking the world and oneself at the same time, by seeing the world and oneself as aesthetic opposites," comprising a cultlike group, eventually to come to ruin). His suicide, at seventy-six, asks: Is the world a broken thing or is it fixed? Is it emptying out toward entropy or caught in constant reconstruction?

Ask kin-tsugi, the Japanese art of "golden joinery," in which a broken bowl is fixed and seamed with glow, cracks to the forefront, filled in by gold, rendering the repaired thing more remarkable, honoring its shatter. The result is neither broken nor unbroken, but both at once, shadow, object, corona around an eclipsed sun.

Own the ways we break, it seems to say: understand that the fault lines of a mind or body are individual, and honor them.

If the outcome seems familiar—that suicide, or breakdown of the nerves, job fuckup, criminal neglect, the colossal choke, ruptured marriage, blown relationship, overmastering of the mind by the body's needs (or the reverse), the ways in which our lives are reduced to their component parts—blame that less on the ways in which we break and more on the ways in which our social selves are told that we might break. We are not so imaginative as we would hope. How did our parents break? How were their parents seared or scarred, weakened then chipped apart by years? And did they still go on, and how? We know so much of their ceaseless weakness but so little of our own.

My brother and I would smash our toys with mallets. We loved the world like this: flattened, trashed. We graduated to car windshields in the field beyond our field where the clunkers came to rest and were swiftly overgrown. A summer venture discovered them, so we came back with rocks and hammers, crowbars and anger to take the things apart. The family barn collapsed in 1977–1978's big winter and decomposed throughout our childhood. My part of Michigan is ruin-strewn. You can't drive twenty miles without finding mining towns abandoned, shafts sunk into rock and given up, covered up or not, derelict steam hoists, brokeback smokestacks, unspooled coils of wire, storm-downed ships, gears like stars in dirt. Then there are the bars with their human wreckage, myself some days among them, oozing all my hot afternoons away. I have some love for you, dear afternoons, warm seams between what my life seemed like and what it is, actual, eventual, inhabiting my father through the books he loves to read, becoming my old self again via teenage marginalia, and now you're putting me on as if a cloak, for a moment, maybe more, running my sentences like lines of code.

You know, though, there's a crack between reading and becoming. One thing is not the other. A seam, it seems, and here it's brought to life. Through it we are aware again of light. We might see the word *light*, too, and be transported to another afternoon, the way we were surprised by how the slowly fading winter sun lit up the men's bathroom on the fourth floor of the building where we work, transformed it into an altar, really, on which we might be asked to sacrifice whatever, and would.

of shadow—but he's writing now, he only has eyes for my friends. Whose names he'll never know but they're alive on his paper, wherever human light and salt are done correctly: my friends are alive. Stein

—Albert Goldbarth, *Different Fleshes* (library of Alison Hawthorne Deming)

In 1999's *Best American Essays,* Edward Hoagland tells us that "essays are how we speak to one another in print . . . in a kind of public letter." Like a numbers station out there broadcasting, he's still telling us. That sentence is still raisined in the brain and seems to be going nowhere. I can't exorcise it. I used it in an essay. I'm using it now in another. That makes it a seed, a panoply.

Dear Albert, I finally got around to reading your strange 1979 poem-novel *Different Fleshes.* I had to borrow Alison Deming's copy, since it's out of print. Hers is filled with marginalia from (she says) 1983. To read another writer's marked-up copy of a book is to read two books at once, text and paratext, the passage and the pilgrim's progress, to see how an animal takes root and begins to worm inside a brain, even if we don't get to see its final bloom. There's no end to the ways that this can shell, reading an essay responding to an essay responding to marginalia on another's essay terminating in a corner of an M. C. Escher drawing, not one of the famous ones.

I didn't always care like this. Look what books have done to me.

You know by now I e-mailed you a decade back. You only know this because I told you via letter, after learning that you never use e-mail, and have, in fact, never touched a computer. Your aversion is not to all technology (after all, the pencil is technology, the box, the essay, the poem, the typewriter, the letter, and the US Mail), since I have your cell phone number in my own phone, a kind of handshake, which we've also shared in the past. I recognize a familiar heart, a collector's heart, a conservator's. In an interview (yes, I read it on the Internet: how do you get by without the quiet hum of connectivity, of near-instant gratification?) you note: "A lot of my own private life is devoted to a sense of conservancy. . . . I conserve objects and ideas in my life. In fact, it hurts me when I see public telephone booths and post office drop-boxes disappearing from the American landscape. Some of my poetry implicitly asks to be a body that freezes some of those objects and the sensibilities they stand for in time. In fact, any poem, whether one wants it to be or not, is necessarily a block of language that to some extent holds firm a group of words and maybe the ideas those groups of words are meant to represent against the depredations of time. To that extent, I think almost any writer is a conservator." Almost any reader too. Though we may love the future in different ways, sir, we read to court the past. But how will you access the library's catalog if you eschew computers?

Dear Alison, at first I found it strange that you underlined this bit: "wherever human / light and salt are done correctly: / my friends are alive." Your marginalia points out the past's presence in the present, an ongoing concern of Albert's book (and of *this* book). In the literary present, anyone we read remains alive. Do you draw my attention to Albert's punctuation in this excerpt? True, a comma would have been the easy choice, but the colon performs a greater prestidigitation: in its longer pause, in the next clause it introduces, in its very act of introduction, its grammatical function (a disruption and conjunction), its small smoke puffs, it summons and resurrects its friends.

Technologies just multiply our hauntings. Thank Derrida for *hauntology,* from the 1983 film *Ghost Dance,* in which he plays himself, a kind of apparition: "Modern developments in technology and communication, instead of diminishing the realm of ghosts, as does any scientific or technical thought, [are multiplying them:] ghosts are part of the future. . . . Modern technology of images like cinematography and telecommunication enhances the power of ghosts and their ability to haunt us." All of this electricity is built on history and often it acknowledges it. Think of our infatuation, in the digital age, with traces of the analog: even *digital* summons *digit,* summons *finger,* that which operates the machine; static and tape deck hiss intrude on contemporary songs as if to respect the past, but often enough they just throw a gesture toward it. A reference is not a resurrection. A sample is not ample to bring it back alive. An image of a book onscreen is not a book. The thing itself retains some meaning, even this late in the evening.

DEAR BOUND

I · · always with I · · one starts from · ·
one and I share the same character · · are one ·
· · · · one always starts with I · · one · ·
· · · alone · · · · · · · · sole · · · ·
· · · · · · · · · single · · · · · · · · · ·
· · I

I have no means of telling, here, down here, when

—B. S. Johnson, *Trawl*, 1966 (PR 6060 O3 T7)

I came looking for *The Unfortunates*, but stumbled on this instead, Johnson's experimental novel *Trawl*. It starts with *I*; one always starts with *I*, even if we try to avoid it, make an ovoid hole in the middle of the page, work a lipogram without the vowel, or begin elsewhere, a found text, perhaps, a page you can almost see through, another underwritten pleasure of the codex book, awareness of the page as object, as doubleness, a thing to be read recto, flipped, then verso, though this ain't an intentional pleasure but a function of its printing, its heavy type, its cheaper paper, the scanner's increased resolution, how it can see through pages, ages. But it's still us looking, us speaking, us opening ourselves up, even if we wear a mask and try real hard to find a life in something else.

Having settled for a different formal excavation than I had intended, I found myself at an end point when I meant beginning. I had hoped to find the barely bound *Unfortunates*, "twenty-seven sections, temporarily held together by a removable wrapper. Apart from the first and last sections (which are marked as such) the other twenty-five sections are intended to be read in random order," according to the author.

What does it mean for a book to operate orderlessly like a closing business? Can a spineless book still be a book? When we say *book* do we just mean *container*? Do we just mean sun around which some crappy planets spin, a gravitation to hold them in, to attach them to an author's name, a myth, a space around which we can hang a world? Or is there something in the way a book, a real one, involves itself with us?

Everything is a carrier. Like words, most deer, whether farmed or wild, carry parasites, echoes of meaning and memory. You can't get rid of them. To be a deer is to be infested. To be a dear is to be infested by another, to be written to, to be addressed, to be remembered. Who taught you that swear first? Who burst your head wide open with a sentence? Whose linguistic tics have you ingested, do you know, bust out without thinking? Best to reconsider what an organism is: not just a self but a collector, a container. Common internal parasites in deer include *Cooperia, Ostertagia, Trichostrongylus, Oesophagostomum,* and *Dictyocaulus viviparus* (lungworm). "Wapiti are especially prone to internal parasites causing severe damage to the stomach lining resulting in a progressive condition called 'Fading Elk Syndrome.'" So a New Zealand vet center says.

In what are we contained? Are we tamed or farmed or wild? Are we systems inside systems, or do we believe ourselves controlled, self-willed containers? There's no way of telling from inside a box like this, a book like this, what an I might look like from outside of it, how awful we look in photographs or how we sound on voicemail, if that's even I we're seeing when we surprise ourselves with a sudden record of our existence, how weird or white or wild or promised to the night it is, that self, whether absence can be a presence, whether the will to fill a space like this is pleasant.

Rain runs all across the city so the streets are briefly washes. It's the monsoon, so suddenly it's here, a microburst, so fast and wild, it blows the trees apart, pleasing the heart with its sexy intensity. Everything's in flux. I know the threat the digital appears to pose to the codex's old technology, but we live in an age of outrage for the sake of it. Perhaps we always have. Then the storm's over and it clears. What was here before is still here. The trees below unbend and stand again, operating as they did before. That sounds like a metaphor.

You've got to be "fucken kidding me! "Nooooooooo..! Greta A lesbian?! I could 'never! have Imagined..oh..My... I've seen dozens of her movies! She's always in love sceens with men!? if she was alive, I bet she would certainly despute this as "Rubbage," and 'sue this Author!

G

Garbo
1990
n actress

arbo was one of the few actors in Hollywood to achieve both silent and talking pictures. Her exotic beauty, her ng ability and professionalism, her androgynous sexual-r mysterious private life made her a star *and* a legend.

born Greta Louisa Gustafson in Stockholm, Sweden, on ber 1905. Her parents, Karl Alfred and Anna Louisa , were so impoverished that they briefly considered al-rl's employer to adopt Greta, the youngest of their three Garbo's father dies when she was 14 years old.

d been starstruck since she was a small child. She loved perform for her family, and dreamed of the theatre. But no money for theatre tickets. Soon after her father's ta took her first job, as a lather-girl in a barbershop. A she became a clerk in the millinery department of a large t store, and then appeared in print ads modeling the s. This led to her first film, *How Not to Dress* (1921), a rtisement for the store.

ng in low-budget films, Greta received minor critical at-r her unusual beauty and comedic talent. By now her a theatrical career was almost an obsession, although she astrated the depression and craving for solitude that would ater life. She overcame her shyness to compete success-scholarship to the Royal Dramatic Theater Academy. v years' maturity and training, she won her first impor-ole in 1924 in an adaptation of Selma Lagerlöf's *Saga of ling*, which became a great European success. This was lm in which she used her stage name, "Greta Garbo."

first important Hollywood film was *The Torrent* (1926), to-Goldwyn-Mayer. It made her a star, praised more for than for her beauty. Over the next four years she ap-ten more silent films, learned to speak English, had her ghtened, and took on a new image fashioned by MGM. e she made her first talking picture, *Anna Christie* (1930), s the embodiment of feminine passion and exotic beauty. several important films in the 1930s, including *Mata Hari* d *Hotel* (1932), *Queen Christina* (1935), *Anna Karenina Camille* (1936) and *Ninotchka* (1939). In these films she ysterious women in glamorous wardrobes; critics found melodramatic, but audiences and other actors adored her. reen, Garbo was far different from the women she played. h the studio arranged to have her photographed as often as on the arms of handsome male stars, she had had several ships with women since the age of 14. Through the 1930s involved with Mercedes de Acosta, a former lover of

Greta Garbo as Mata Hari *Gretta Garbo is "NOT" A Lesbian—"Noo—way!"*

Marlene Dietrich; Garbo and de Acosta would remain on-again-off-again lovers and friends for 40 years. When not working, Garbo wore wide-shouldered suits with trousers, an unusual look for women at the time. MGM would not permit her to wear pants in her films because it would counter the studio's carefully crafted feminine image. But the public became accustomed to seeing newspaper and magazine photos of her in pants, and found the combination of androgynous off-screen image and ultra-feminine on-screen image intriguing.

Among friends, Garbo enjoyed playing the role of a man, and being addressed as "sir." As her power at the studio increased, Garbo lobbied MGM for films in which she could play male char-acters, including Hamlet and Dorian Gray. But her efforts were unsuccessful.

In 1941 Garbo starred in the disastrous *Two-Faced Woman*. She was unhappy throughout the filming, and never acted again, in spite of several offers of choice roles. Retired at the age of 36, she became a recluse, almost as famous in subsequent decades for her mysteri-ous isolation as for her films. In 1954 she was awarded a special

Lies!..Lies!..LIES..!

—*Gay & Lesbian Biography*, ed. Michael J. Tyrkus (HQ 75.2 G39 1997, University of Arizona Library, Main)

In truth I too defaced—books, surely, furiously, variously, before I understood their worth; but also: walls, homes, computer systems, aboveground pools, school buses, schools, school desks and lockers, bathroom stalls, urinals, garage doors, a bus station, car glass, cars, glass block windows, wine glasses at parties, Mr. Millenbach's shed. The list embarrasses but I need to say it: my name or my words are carved in or written all over, in margins of all sorts, on borrowed sports equipment, even, in the evening. Was this an evening out of anything, restoring a sense of balance, scoring, settling? Was it about power? Feeling my breath, my reach, effect linked to cause, a pausing of the world in order to press myself into it, adolescent, and leave it marked?

Dear Defacer, this is a book about the margin, so while the librarians surely won't, I welcome your marginalia, since it starts to arc, suggest your story, growing worry about gender, sex. It starts in stutter: bitchassery: a variety of slurs, faggot this, lesbo that, a yawn, you burring anyone you can, pathological, uncontrolled. A hundred pages later your shriek against how easy it must be to come out when you're rich betrays a shadow self. The pool's shallow end is not so shallow as it seems, or else you're drowning there regardless (they say it only takes an inch).

On a later page your confession of your age makes the action weirder. Then: "Should I really be aware that Oscar Wild [sic] is queer? or was?" Yes, you should, if you're in your sixties, as you say, if you've read. "If I had never known Oscar Wild [sic] was a faggot why the fuck does someone have to tell me after 100 fuckn years?" You may have noticed we're in the *Gay & Lesbian Biography*. Why else were you here?

I'm not sure it's fair to pair the two of us, Defacer: sixteen is a life away from sixty-six, but still I want to understand your small, weird heart. Our anger suggests our sadness, that the sum of us in misdirected screeds is greater than the part.

Don't we all wear our faces loosely? Is it sad to say our eyes are masks?

Garbo's face a mask. Emily Dickinson's, as you complain. Wilde's. Ma Bell's, you note, though you know she's even less real than the rest of these. Your face a mask. My face a mask. This book a mask. Your marks in it, masks. Each mask a mask. These sentences a mask, red death, a self-photographed macaque, a walk through the history of our error-prone approach to sex, desire, to gender, fashion, film: these things are kilns in which we bake the masks of self anew. These things are stones upon which we are asked to dash each mask each evening in order to keep breathing.

you Know". There is Anothing to, people who are rich, or maybe not rich and famous yet, tend to wait until they are really well known and have a billion dollars in the bank before They come out and say "I'm GAY" or I'm a Lesbian." They talk about all this "be proud of who you are shit! but when nobody knows you, you hide who you are. And if your nobody — yes you say I'm Gay "I'll march in the-parade, but if your a GAY singer, And only have one C.D. out and not really Nationally Accl— Aimed yet? fuck yeah! your gonna hide your true self — because money means more to you Then loosing everything beacause you said: IM GAY". before you [279] have your $50.000 Lambrighini"

—*Gay & Lesbian Biography*, ed. Michael J. Tyrkus (HQ 75.2 G39 1997, University of Arizona Library, Main)

A signal does not necessarily mean that you want to be located or described. It can mean that you want to be known as Unlocatable and Hidden.

—Fanny Howe, "Bewilderment"

I've been thinking more about silence and signal, how we're viewed, you and I, how we take in the world, what we say about it, on which subjects can we just not ever hold our tongues. Wondering if I put too much of myself in the world, whether this set of selves I offer you opens me up too far. I know I can't take it back—what I wrote, what I said. It exists in small ways on and between pages, in private collections and public collections, intentionally and not. It exceeds me, the myth I make (the myth readers construct of authors—what we believe about those who write the things we love), like how some perceive RealDolls or avatars, characters in games or books. An author is even better: she made this thing your brain tangles with. Is reading her work like knowing her? Like loving her? Of course, I don't know who holds me in their hands today, who gathers my brain in their own and rubs it, how long and what for.

Dear Defacer, you won't hold me in your hands, I'm sure, since most of your books have been removed along with your voice, such as it is. You're banned from the university library because you did a felony amount of damage to the books and shelves (we pause this programming for an interrobang: ?) and maybe selves of those who came to these books for answers, insight, communion, community. That your anger was made manifest less than six months before the shooting of our congresswoman Gabrielle Giffords suggests an easy meaning, that this is hate, not speech, that we differentiate the two, that this sort of hate can lead, infused by gun availability, to tragedy. Yes, it's a gap between vandalism and domestic terrorism, but the rage is there, the aggression there, the delusion there. You've extended that part of yourself, even if we prefer to read it as self-directed. Talking back suggests your fear, that you understand you're being spoken to in here. I know enough of anger that it means something has hit your heart and got it firing. Surely it's not just pathology, stimulus and odd response. Like this, your accusation of the authors (filed under Wilde): "you're a fucking big mouth with nothing else better to do but gossup [sic] about everyones [sic] past or present sexual history." Their collection and inclusion here are political, Defacer. Perhaps that's what you're responding to.

But isn't that what humans do? We want to know. We like to hear. We trade in gossip. We want to build a heart out of what we have in front of us, to know how and why and when and for how long they worked, what forces drove them, what made them do what they did, why they built a wall, why they tore it down.

For those seeking safety in these pages, you've ruined that. Instead we find a threat, a pissing match with no one. Does your assertion make you happy? We live in a society, though sometimes it doesn't feel like much of one. Still, I want to know your name, what makes you go, why you play this strange.

Now This—"being a man" does look quite

if I WAS drunk enough —yeah—

might Just fuck him

GAY & L

ul

·American female impersonator and singer

Andre Charles was born in 1960, the only son in a family
women. It is to the strong women in his life that RuPaul
his love of the feminine principle. He grew up in San
developed a fascination with the theatre early in life. His
in to drag occurred when a girlfriend took him to see *The*
ror Picture Show and when, in 1978, he met his first drag

—*Gay & Lesbian Biography*, ed. Michael J. Tyrkus (HQ 75.2 G39 1997,
University of Arizona Library, Main)

At last, puzzled to comprehend the meaning of such a knot, Captain
Delano addressed the knotter: "What are you knotting there, my
man?"

"The knot," was the brief reply, without looking up.

"So it seems; but what is it for?"

"For someone else to undo," muttered back the old man, plying his
fingers harder than ever, the knot being now nearly completed.

—Herman Melville, *Benito Cereno*

Then let's start with impersonation and biology, two knots that concern RuPaul:
they concern you too, Defacer. These knotted balls implicate us all (are we what
or who we're predisposed to be?), complications looped through complications.
What's interesting is that in spite of what you know—that he's a man and prefers
you refer to him as he—because, as he claims, biology matters—you might just
fuck him if you were drunk enough.

A day after finding this, a student writes in a critique that everything is sex. Most
days I'm not so sure. Is your world made up of the fuckable and not, Defacer, two
lines knotted, so that every moment is a verdict? Is this how your knot of heart

must be expressed, as primal body urge, as missed connection, solo male seeking something temporary, unoriginal? In what ways are you lonely, dear Defacer, to put so much of yourself in this space? Do you need someone in your life, another face to rage against, another heart to mirror, enter, and untangle?

I am trying to imagine you, Defacer, but you remain a cipher. The police can't locate your incident report. So you remain unnamed, unfaced, unplaced, unbound, except in books not your own.

Do you believe you are yourself when you are drunk, or are you someone else? Are you freer then? I imagine your body heavy in this chair, where, by error, I found this evidence of your hidden heart, that second space we more rarely open, as scrawled all across this book. Anonymity makes us bold, Defacer. I understand. Some of us can only expose ourselves to strangers.

I imagine you as troll, here to irritate all comers from your location raging underneath the bridge. I imagine you as bully: difficult to defend yourself against a ghost. I imagine you as medieval scribe, illuminating texts. But the final heart inside the other hearts (I know that I am here imagining you as game, as text, as enigma, layer cake, as concentric, stacked, geodesic domes, each one smaller, harder, more and more like ore than the last) is as confessor, unintentional: write long enough and hard enough into the space past waking or attention and you find yourself unspooling. Good reason to engage the hypnopompic or hypnagogic states, emerging from sleep or leading backward into it, to discover what's underneath the sea of who we think we are.

The space between biology and biography is vast. Both are tests. They seek to understand a life. We might believe we write our own, that who we think we are gives us the right to tell ourselves as we believe we are. The telling of a self is fiction too, salesmanship, however unintentional, how in narrating I we change the I—we make it harder, stellar, starlike, more like shell than skin, how we hide all evidence to the contrary, believe ourselves impermeable.

Is that why you were here, to work your heart against a mirror series? RuPaul's not me, you seem to say, and you can't find me here or anywhere. Yet in this annotation you two are paired, knotted up. *Not you* still invokes the *you*, even if we wonder who and what and how and why you really are.

> Emy Dikinson coub've ne'r struck me a lesbian!
> DICKINSON Now This Just "CONFIRMS" it. to GAY & LESBIAN BIOGRAPHY
> Bad—I wAs Somewhat fond of her books" BEFORE!

time of Emily's birth, the family was then living at the Homestead, a house which had been built in 1814 by Edward's father, Samuel Fowler Dickinson, who would move to Ohio in 1833. Edward's own rise in the Amherst community was signalled by his appointment in 1835 as treasurer of Amherst College, and in 1838 he began his first term in the Massachusetts General Court. He sold his half-share of the Homestead in 1840 and moved his family to a nearby house on Mount Pleasant Street. In September of that year, Dickinson and her younger sister entered the co-educational Amherst Academy.

Dickinson's first intense and intimate friendship was with Sophia Holland, whom she idolized but who died when Dickinson was 14. Dickinson's *Letters* record that she wrote of Sophia: "[s]he was too lovely for earth." In 1844, she began another intense friendship with Abiah Root, then herself a student at Amherst Academy. Although Abiah left after a year to go to Springfield Academy, Dickinson continued to write lovingly to her until 1856, the year in which Abiah married and stopped replying to Emily's letters. In

. . . Being as pretty as she looks—I'da ne'r guessed

—Marginalia, *Gay & Lesbian Biography*, ed. Michael J. Tyrkus
(HQ 75.2 G39 1997, University of Arizona Library, Main)

Like Emily, you too seem to love the dash, even if you don't deploy it well— your diminutive for her is unwarranted, too—what sounds your heart made inside a room, reading her for instance—I wonder, have you ever really read her or do you just know the name—and if you'd read her what did you think of her work—not just her countenance—or how you perceived her sex—or orientation toward or away from you—the world doesn't care for you as much as you seem to care for it—I hate to tell you this—even if it hurts your twit-heart a little bit— but how you write suggests you know—so do you think your words a signal— like shortwave radio—a microphone you speak into every night—even if you rarely are acknowledged—is your speech a confession to the world—or an interrogation of it—in the way nights in Tucson—a "dark city"—meaning streetlights are restricted—meaning porch lights are restricted—meaning night here is darker than anyplace you've ever known—for the astronomers who work an hour or so away—in places like Kitt Peak—or atop Mount Lemmon—somewhat closer to the stars—and a bit beyond the city light-leak haze—that takes place in spite of our attempts—to curtail the way we spread—and so the night is bigger, wider, deeper—more of it to speak your little heart into—to fire your anger into like a signal—instead of books you might try this—a microphone, a call sign, a homemade kit—it doesn't take much—to get yourself heard—if that's what you're wanting here—if that's what you're waiting for—Dickinson of course projected far beyond her home—in spite of her seclusion—and is still radiating out toward stars—sad to say it feels unthinkable in the American Internet Reality now—not to court the light—in fact to shy away from it—but still to make such work—such words as hers—which it's a shame to even try—to compare to yours—or to parse formally—in this way, a minor karaoke—of the mouth and heart—maybe instead we should sing—"The Battle Hymn of the Republic"—as performed by Warrant—it's easy to forget them—cock-rockers, middle of the pack at best—but still—how "Sometimes She Cries"—which I'm listening to at the moment—exemplar of the confusing era of the power ballad—released in 1990, near the end of that rock era—and the lead singer's deeply terrible hat in the video—his stage name was Jani Lane—his birth name John Kennedy Oswald—an awful combination—a signal of unapproachability or unlocatability perhaps—his given name, stage name, his hat—he died in 2011—of alcohol poisoning—after failing to revive an alternate version of Warrant—at forty-seven—which leads me to, in honor of Dickinson—of Lane—of you, anonymous Defacer—of you, reader—to cue this up for karaoke—next Friday night at the Royal Sun Best Western—and every Friday after that—until all the lights go dark—and/or the stars go out.

If this is your philosophy of life
Help spread the "Golden Key" among children
Valley of the Moon . . . . BULLETIN

—Arizona Historical Society, Valley of the Moon Collection (MS 828, box 1, folder 8)

You're speaking but not listening, Defacer. Turns out that, according to the library, you were apprehended but not charged because they didn't catch you in the act. But still you're here inside the folds of books, inside my folds of brain. Maybe you're my Minotaur, angry, frenzied, charging, pissing, marking up the walls, part man, part not. What I wish was that I could ask you questions and you could answer about your heart and what it holds and what you mean to do with it.

But they won't tell me your name. Discretion is more than you deserve. Or maybe you deserve to have your name erased from every library, your card revoked, your account erased from the database. You tried hard to put your words into the world, and I suppose you have. Perhaps in reproducing them I multiply your force. Possibly I see my adolescent self diminished in your scrawl. But I can't just shrug you off. You are a darkness that I need to better know.

Astronomers call it *averted vision:* to see a thing sometimes you have to avert your view, just enough to let your charge emerge. It's what they say of fairyfolk or sprites, the sort that the spiritualists believed in not so long ago. Just five miles away we could go, you and I, to the Valley of the Moon, a relic of another age, a pre-Disneyland spiritualist fantasy for kids, now run down, but still in operation. Created by George Phar Legler in the 1920s as a shrine to the worlds inhabited by kids before they're bent into adults, it was his life's work, a monument to wonder. A retired postal clerk, a carrier of others' messages from sender to receiver, he believed this place would be a message to the future via children: "If we can influence children to develop a friendly attitude toward everyone while they are children they will be happier adults. That friendly attitude will unconsciously react on their subconscious minds and, in turn, will strengthen their characters and give them deeper spiritual outlooks in life regardless of what church they may ultimately belong to."

He called himself the Mountain Gnome. He built the Valley mostly by himself. A spiritualist, he believed he could nearly touch the other through the ether:

31

faeries, spirits, beasts, magnetism, radio, a world beyond the one we see and feel. He spoke to it through us, or to us through it. For the last decades of his life he lived alone in a cave in the Valley, sustained exclusively by milk, imagination, and "thirteen kinds of pills" according to an article in *Life*. He would take no money from visitors.

Legler died in 1982, though through his place he feels to me alive. To each of his children and his wife, he left exactly $100, which isn't much, but then the world he cared for went beyond the material. The rest of his estate, such as it was, he left to volunteers, the George Phar Legler Society, many of whom visited the site as children, their names (until 1953 when he for some reason ceased) inscribed in the hotel register he used as a guestbook. Did you come here when you were young, Defacer? Did you sign his book? Are you one of them? I looked therein for traces of your hand, hoping to find your name, but you would have been very young if you came at all.

I saw no trace of your hand. I'm inclined to believe you never made it here. What was your childhood like, Defacer? In your adult scrawl I can feel you struggling to emerge—and when you do you manifest as rage, by-product of the complaining age.

Dear Defacer, I know it's tough to suspend our disbelief like this, gnarled, hardened, modern as we believe we are. Still perhaps it's not too late to rehabilitate your heart, the echo chamber of your voice. It's your choice. If you'd go, I would take you to the Mystic Pool; the Tower of Zogog, where the wizard lives; the Gnome Village; the Canyon of the Writhing Serpent Monster; and if you would not speak to me I'd leave you there in its clutches and bid you listen hard.

Whom do we speak to, and how do we encode our messages? How can we be heard or read, even after we are dead?

Fraternally yours,
Mountain Gnome,
2544 East Allen Road,
Tucson, Arizona.

I wonder what my philosophy of life really is and if I am doing anything for my fellow men for the privilege of sharing their society.

—Jean Baudrillard, *The System of Objects* (BF 778.B313, 1996, IN LIBRARY)

Found: this book, or its record, since the book was lost into the space between IN LIBRARY and DUE 03-10-13, according to the machine that holds the ghosts of what was formerly a catalog of manmade cards in drawers, and its   from the shelf that should hold its spine. Some books are taken accidentally or are otherwise disappeared, misplaced, misshelved, mutilated, bent, spindled, fed to sharks, used as kindling out of desperation, stolen for prurient purposes, defaced then deleted from the catalog, or shoved in the wrong stack on the wrong cart for eventual reshelving by a human. That the book—this book, *The System of Objects*—itself was   but the computer record still signified its presence pleases: the system fails; the object's missing; the world is not so orderly as we might imagine. Instead: a space. Braces on each side if you can use your imagination. My ardor. A tear in the order. Monk away without leave, never to come back. Nothing in the book to find, since no book to find. Just my stupid expectation: how long have I relied on the memory of the machine instead of my own?

A week later—after I scrambled the librarians in desperation, the system responds: "We were unable to get availability information for this item." Another week, the book arrives via interlibrary loan, but I can't erase its   . It's hard to get Baudrillard's heady text into my texty head; it's dense, tense to read, difficult to parse, but produces this: "the passion for objects . . . produces the urge to sequester beauty so as to be the only one to enjoy it: a kind of sexually perverse behaviour widely present in a diffuse form in the relationship to objects" (98). Desire is a desire to contain, constrict, apply form to by collection, by compression.

On the desk by the computer that accesses the catalog, there is a box of quartered card catalog cards, blank on the back, to be marked with call numbers to transport those numbers to the stacks where the numbers—if the scrawl permits—might lead a reader to a book, if the book is there. I took all the quartered cards in the box. I covet their oddness. And who wouldn't? It's hard not to love them, the million remnants of the transition to machine. There's always been a disconnect between the catalog and the stacks, cracks in the model wall sometimes so as to produce an undergraduate wail if you stay there long enough and quietly, usually followed by a fury of texting words into machines or speaking words into a telephone that cuts off the top and bottom frequencies of the human voice, reduces its meaning-making part into a bandwidth suitable for error-free transmission via wire, threaded glass, or air. Soon we'll find we're emptinesses too—disembodied, our voices sexless, our tresses shorn, our skulls hairless, our barely legal genitalia bare so as for better display onscreen or to correlate more perfectly with the porn we've normed ourselves to every night just after our lovers go to sleep, permanently unsatisfied or   .

Who we are when we're online is another   . We're filled with blanknesses. Are our hearts somehow more bare when we exist as avatar? Even a name, screen name, handle, title, nom de plume is avatar. Who or what we are, we represent. We resent when the system fails: when the Internet slows to a trickle and then stops, when we drop frames, black-hole e-mails, when we can't find the porn we stashed away, when the books we are assured are there are not in fact, are effectively nowhere, like blank tape hiss, like dial tone, like dropped call, mislaid connection. We wonder what good is a collection anyway if we can't have it when we want it, if we can't contain it in a form.

p. 23, l. 16	for 2.2	read 3.2
p. 39, l. 24	for 25	read 26
p. 45, top	for middle ages	read ancient times
p. 46, l. 7 in note	for parapetted	read parapeted
p. 54, l. 11	for Fig.	read Figs.
p. 54, l. 21	for size	read length
p. 54, l. 24	for Imole	read Imola
p. 57, l. 4	for San	read Sant'
p. 57, l. 7	for 1.8	read 1.6
p. 94, l. 16	for delle Erbe	read dell' Erbe
p. 222, last l.	for Borbini	read Borboni
Plate 19, l. 8	for Paletine	read Palatine
Plates 35 and 39	for Peranesi	read Piranesi
Plate 89, l. 8	for Giovannie	read Giovanni
Plates 120, 122, 127	for Sepulcre	read Sepulchre
Plate 142	for Gacte	read Gaeta
Plate 146	for Cappocci	read Capocci

—G. C. Mars, ed., *Brickwork in Italy*, American Face Brick Association, 1925
(NA iiii A4, Wilko Library)

Bound into the edition, post-press, an errata card blooms from a blank spread. Such authority! The publisher—or the writer—or the editor—cares this much about the details, so necessary was it to correct "parapetted" to "parapeted," both of which spellcheck redlines as wrong, though the latter is in fact correct. More important errors are those of inspecificity ("middle ages" instead of "ancient times") or the wrong measure ("size" instead of "length"). I love errata sheets for how they acknowledge error and correct it. They do not erase. In the hour of digital, when something disappears it leaves little trace, convenient but a cause for concern, since our errors also are individual, mineral, DNA-stained. Not all are meaningful, but some might be, for instance when in 1998 I offered a student a cookie and she misheard it as a quickie? What we want and what we admit to wanting are held apart only some days by mindfulness or conscious thought. It's how we are, Italian brickwork, hair gel, light conversation, surface tension, holding ourselves in with whatever we can. Some days it's just Saran Wrap, which, though it's found these days in kitchens, was first used on combat boots and fighter planes before being turned into the clingy gloss that once bespoke the future, one of plastics rolled or sprayed on everything to keep world and time from food and self.

We knew then our food would never spoil. We'd never run short of oil or tire of it or saturate the earth with chemical spill. We could hold everything in with technology: an errata page holds the wall against time and human error. What else is a library but a history of human error, one thought about the world installed after the one before, a series of approximations, reconsidered, repurposed? Will any of them last? It's a misspelling to get from the wrap to sarin gas, named from an acronym of its four discoverers (Schrader, Ambros, Rüdiger, and Van der Linde— the Germans discovered it in 1938 as a pesticide and subsequently incorporated it into artillery shells). It's highly volatile, mixes easily with water, contaminates food; "a person's clothing can release sarin for about 30 minutes after it has come into contact with sarin vapor," according to the CDC. The latency of an idea, luckily, is far longer.

Saran Wrap, once made of polyvinylidene chloride (PVDC), is now polyethylene instead, due to "environmental concerns with halogenated materials" (incineration on disposal released dioxins). PVDC is still used "for high-quality doll hair that is valued by collectors for its shine, softness, and its ability to retain its style and curl." Once we were alive, then we weren't. We thought ourselves wild, apart from world; our hair still curled, more than just a chemical collection. Then we were erased. If we're lucky, we left a trace.

—Thomas A. Stein and H. Douglas Sessoms, *Recreation and Special Populations*
(GV 171.S78 C.02, University of Arizona Science & Engineering Library)

Here's a relic for the reliquary. Another artifact of the past. Go ahead, take it, collect it, chuck it: it no longer serves its former function. I find them still with regularity in academic libraries, in the science and engineering sections, in books that may themselves be obsolete or just past their sell-by date (like the above, from 1977). Still, for nearly two centuries these cards have served! I put them in a box with the gears I found in the wreckage of the burned-down barn when I was young.

Printed cards seem an odd choice for a technology to be computer read. These days we think of one as the other's foe: electronic book and printed book; electronic journal and printed journal; digital and photograph; the eighteenth century's chess-playing automaton, the Mechanical Turk (which defeated both Napoléon and Ben Franklin in games of chess) and Amazon's Turk, a "Marketplace for Work." But it wasn't always so: before magnetic storage, the punch card was the preferred medium for the digital.

Now a card functions only as a screen: place it over text to see which letters its holes reveal, a few lit rooms in a building at night, seen from the street, featuring an indifferent woman removing clothes, draping them across a chair. All technologies are just a screen: you either look at what's behind the tech, what it reveals, how the world is edited down in this way to these few openings (this is what a window or an aperture is good for), or you illuminate the surface you are looking through and give it your attention.

Jacquard looms used punched cards as far back as 1810 to control the weaving pattern (and these looms—these cards—are still used by a few today, in Amana, Iowa, for instance), though they didn't become instructions for machines we call computers until the 1950s.

Still, its rhetoric is shrill: DO NOT LOSE. How close are we to losing it, neck sunk in now and the urge for more of it: new gadgetry, technology, efficiency. I like all these, of course, but the edge advances. Soon what we cherished a decade back may be unreadable: try to find a drive to read your floppy disks. Burned CDs might last a decade, maybe less. Then there's the glory of the cloud until it storms and lightning spikes the server or the user.

Sad half an iPhone I found on the curb while walking with my wife: once you too were new and promised much. Now you're metallic mulch.

We notice that our new machines—ultralight laptops reading and uploading data to our servers—work like our old machines—terminals reading and uploading data to our servers. In between we had a little burst of self-sufficiency.

Savor the technologies we have. Thumb their ergonomic surfaces, their lovely screens, the paper weave as you turn a page. Take pleasure in how they operate. The smooth dials of the stereos I grew up with. The craggy surfaces of the essay, a technology for thinking, an artificial intelligence. The hush of a good pencil along a white sheet. My stenographer's pad, acknowledging its anagram, reads *Steno | Notes*. My book still reads fine in bath, in sun, not plugged in.

Consider the aperture card, a punch card with a sheet of microfilm inset, a fuse of analog and digital. Created in 1943 by Film 'N File, it still persists: a 2004 white paper reports "35mm Aperture Cards — Very Much Alive! . . . [They continue] to have a storage shelf life of over 100 years where magnetic, CD-ROM, and other digital storage media's [*sic*] have a maximum shelf life of 7–25 years." Since we're so poor at reckoning with what comes next, it might be best to hedge our bets (a phrase is a technology, too: this persists from the sixteenth century, in which one hedged one's land to secure it, to limit risk), not to bet the hedge and the land entire.

—H. M. Dowsett, *Wireless Telephony and Broadcasting*, 1924
(University of Arizona Science & Engineering Library)

How old will you be when you are able to read this page? When you care enough to spend your time with things like this, if ever? By grace and luck and the old gods I hereby exhort to stay their random hands, I hope to be here to see what the future is with you inside it, how it holds you like we are all held in the warm arms of our eras, their tragedies, and their technologies.

That you exist is proof enough the world is not yet an entirely ruined place. It might still turn out to be. I cannot know. But I believe, for what it's worth, like those who gaze at stars or those who turn their lenses inward and inwarder still toward our electron hearts to see what moves inside them. There must be something there.

This is why I'm writing you, our small star of future lover, our Scylla and Charybdis, our future reader, our two-liter Vernors drinker, our future fat American, syntactical construction, beast of blood and fire and wail and grunt and eye. I write to lament the speed and the availability of things. I write to exclaim and celebrate the speed and availability of things, their expanding much-ness and seeming everpresence. We can contain both hearts, I hope.

Cricketsound. The scent of palo verde. The algorithmic blink of search. Car lights in the night across the cave wall, seen just through the blinds. What do they illuminate except for this, this lonely second, this half a cul-de-sac? It's all we have, the lonely seconds, and what thoughts we can fit inside their girth. I hope that you can make yourself a space alone with words. I wrote my mother in another card. She hasn't been alive for many years. It's too much to expect that these or any words can find her there, wherever she is, if she is in a where at all, if those words might open up whatever boundary separates this world from the next. If I believed myself capable of that I would do nothing else for at least a year. Still part of me must still believe in the permeability of membranes between one human heart, one lifespan, and another. Otherwise I would not read books.

I do believe in a world after this one, even if it's just yours or those you've opened up to it or shared it with. I am no sentimentalist. I am no survivalist, but I'd like to survive. I have been an onanist on occasion. Though unlike the Onan of Genesis I have not had sex with my sister-in-law after my brother's death so as to procreate and fulfill the commandment of my god. I hope it doesn't come to that.

The loss of things. A species a minute. A book a second.

Dear future lover, sometimes I can see the order; I can feel it humming under-neath the syntax like a vine, an electric line. Connections everywhere—this sen-tence a nexus of carsound and a touch of cloud, my mortality, the ways in which we are animal, the ways in which we're not. We're something else, we're plus (we hope and cannot know).

Something's working underneath the world. I just can't parse it, yet I know it's there. My diminished hair, the books of Cortázar, an hour spent contemplating the hearts of stars. This is the way I pray, to the gods of order, the gods of col-lection, of cataloging and cross-referencing, the gods of three stars aligning in an essay, the gods of open skies and those who count and sort the clouds, the snow, or other weather, the gods of preservation, the sentence gods and those who sen-tence us to keep composing under penalty of irrelevance or despair, and to those who watch over books, these brittle things that contain our best attempts.

In your handling of these matters, your thoughtfulness will be appreciated.

Everyone who is not from here
is *not from here*, and that is all there is to say.
Everyone from here is still from here
regardless of where they are or where they end.

—Ander Monson, *Vacationland* (811.6 MON, Portage Lake District Library)

A bright surprise to find my first book in the first library I remember haunting as a child, searching for some way out of all this snow, like a closing loop. I'm honored to be a presence here, no matter how small or how long I go between reads. I've thought a lot about this place. Even if it's moved a couple of blocks now toward the water, it serves my people, and so it has my heart.

To live in a place like this is to inhabit absence—or its perception, since it's flyover to some, unpopulated, a dearth, a cultural abyss, a blank space on the map. They don't know how a blank like this can still be full, lush, how it can contain a life. If they knew how our sort of cold can brighten up your heart and remind you that you are alive, then they would be here. We are glad they're not.

Growing up this far north I was not aware that we had a literature, that anyone had written of this place, this peninsula. After all, we are made of whiteness with our endless nights of snow and ice sculptures and ice fishing and our hush of winter silence.

Living here you come to understand the silence is not so silent: there are the sounds of creaking wood in blizzard wind and the sibilance of soft snow through pines on moonlit nights. That exact sound is what I miss the most: to be in the trees not far from home as snow drifts slowly down. Then there are the interior pleasures: a breath-catch from the one you love, or the dying fire and a reminder of your loneliness. Hold on to it, that loneliness, that aloneness. Use it as a fuel.

I had to leave, but still I carry it. You carry this place too even if you do not know it yet. Call it your donnée, what you're given, whether you choose to examine it or not. You may have to leave to understand just how unusual it is and how to polish it like stones.

Consider our word *pank:* to pank is to flatten (to pat, to spank down) snow so as to walk on it more easily without snowshoes, because there's far too much to be moved or shoveled or erased (my father would remind me that we never *shovel* snow up here: we only *move* it). That is, we use what covers us—what interferes—what erases—that which we are given—that which is inclement and other—to build and to traverse, to make some noise, to make some meaning, maybe. In this way absence becomes a presence. You can make yourself a presence too. We can ink with white. It's not just the color of the page for another's type.

And are we panked in turn, compressed down into ourselves? By what forces and for how long?

If I could duplicate this card and make it inexhaustible I would.

So take this note home. Write and insert another in its stead. What might you want—or need—anonymously or not (though I'd say sign your name if you can bear it)—to say to the next reader? To someone you love? To someone you hope one day to be worthy of? Make something from what you're given.

In truth I tell you that daily visits to museums, libraries, and academies (cemeteries of empty exertion, Calvaries of crucified dreams, registries of aborted beginnings!) are, for artists, as damaging as the prolonged super-vision by parents of certain young people drunk with their talent and their ambitious wills.

—F. T. Marinetti, "The Founding and Manifesto of Futurism 1909,"
in *Futurist Manifestos,* ed. Umbro Apollonio (NX 600 F8 A6513 copy 2,
University of Arizona Science & Engineering Library)

I'm all for fast, have always been, the speed of information never fast enough: modem handshake tying up the only family line, slow download protocol impeding acquisition of whatever I felt I just must have right now. Yes, now. I know it's dumb that how I want it but I want it want it. But then that now is gone, and I'm still here. A year transpires. Another. Like you, I hope, I've learned the fruitful wait, the troll through stacks for books I cannot find online and have delivered through the air.

A library is a synonym for slow, a silent coil into the past's dust. Quick transmission of anything here won't get you anywhere. Or: it'll get you where it turns out others have been before. So it's always been. The end of youth is the end of proclamations such as this. (Though, just in case, I hereby retain the right to proclaim or lament the future as I see necessary, in whatever terms.) The growth of information takes years, is gradual, accumulative. It's okay. So to access these manifestos on speed, art, being, and a not incidental misogyny that needs mentioning, here's where you're found, Marinetti, in the library that you lament.

The Futurist Cookbook is shelved among the cookbooks in the basement. An irony of history, then, to be so archived with all the other waves of avant-garde, shelved leisurely in academic libraries with the treatises on art that you dismissed. That these avant-gardes have passed suggests the speed of obsoletion: first you feel you're on the edge of something, then it shifts, that moment's gone, and there's just your histrionics.

"Damage noted 11-06-89," a librarian's note reads—on the sleeve where the punch card used to go. That was the future, too, room-sized machines to calculate just how quickly we might perambulate the stacks, cogitating how to push the future leeward. Just a little shift would do. As in space, one nudge will prompt a drift. So the happenstance of water-damaged books, these old ghosts sentenced to the future here, creates an accidental art, collage of tear and obscured text. I like to think the reader who caused the spill was so suffused by speed and your exhortations toward lust and recklessness and fury, the necessarily aggressive action of good art, that she splashed coffee across the page and left it there—a wet corrosion, a response. You slowed eventually, Marinetti. You surely found the future's faster yet than you had dreamed. You'll slow too, future reader, futurist. And then you'll join me here, father, figure, water feature on the lawn, guest of the age or a ghost of the one before. I'll meet you where the future meets the past.

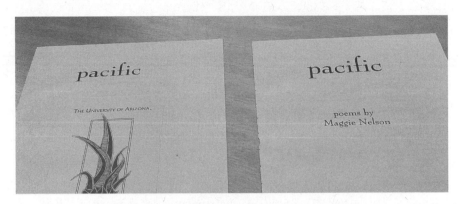

—Maggie Nelson, *Pacific*, Orchard Street Press, 1995
(University of Arizona Poetry Center Library, 22,775)

The book, which I think you made or had made on your behalf, unwinds as I open the cover, pages falling out, as if to say, here, I am a book, but only barely, and not even in a box! It's fall, though down here there are few trees unleafing. Instead, a series of dudes at desks, all nodding sagely, rapt, their hands on books. No one but me is watching this occur. The smell of milling barley comes from somewhere—not from here: we don't grow it here, I'm sure—so from memory, maybe, a new grain dream like the sort I've been having on my low-carb, wheat-free "Primal Blueprint" diet in which I have increasingly come to want to be chain-fucked by varieties of Doritos I haven't ever seen before on earth: Cheesegasm; Doppler Rush; Tastes Like Stacy, Maybe; Sudden Memory Extreme; Everything Will Now Taste Bland All Week; Evanescent Orange; Molesting Double Gloucester; Defibrillator for Your Cheating Heart; Recombination of Already Existing Flavors; Leftover Whatever; Extreme Squeal; Taco Chump/Champion; the American South; So Much for Your Mouth. You know the kind. It's new. It's Huge. It pairs—not well—with wine.

I know this book's unmaking is not intentional. Some pages are held by glue from 1995. It was book number 22,775 acquired, since this library eschews Dewey and the Library of Congress system. Maggie, I am sad to say this book is not well made (no saddle-stitch, no stitch of any sort, a bit of faulty glue the only mechanism holding page to spine), so it falls apart. I don't know, Orchard Street Press, do you exist or are you a shell, Dorito standing in for something else beyond Dorito? Are you asking me to take a page, then another, knowing I can't take just one? A TV commercial for Lay's potato chips circa 1967 says "Bet You Can't Eat

Just One," and features Bert Lahr, the Cowardly Lion from *The Wizard of Oz*, as both himself and the devil. In so doing, I might make *Pacific* mine, two pages at a time, reducing it to just its shell, a title page and table of contents, successfully disambiguated from its contents. In this way my life is spent, accumulating slowly, contents having settled during transport.

Books like this give the lie to form. It's not their fault. It's ours. It's so easy to forget these are technologies: they're read but also made; they disappear into the brain but still persist past our best intentions. A poem gets converted to emotion, maybe a remembered couplet, some excitements: linguistic, sexual, intellectual, just the edges of memories of my reading. It holds our old selves in the creases, in the way the dog-eared pages settle on the shelf; our breath, our disappearing skin dusts the margins. It's easy to forget we're made of juice and electricity; membrane, fluid; male, female, and the electricity in between; Wonderbra and Spanx; systole and diastole. When we rupture we too disintegrate. Those we love keep bits of us, the best of us, we hope, but then there's the other stuff that we'd as soon forget.

Later, as I think again of this disintegrating book two librarians get into it around the corner, just past the last card catalog in another library a half a mile away. They imagine they can't be overheard, that their systems do not intersect with ours. As I listen it starts to fall apart. I only hear half of half the conversation: *It was only fifteen minutes. I let you know. Okay. Right. You fucking liar. I know. We all have to do it. Yes, I'm the biggest. . . . I'm saying, you've seen it. I'm the biggest hypocrite. This is totally off the record. Are you saying—I want you to feel—Who said that? Who said that? That's what I'm talking about. I'm not blaming—I'm not putting this on you. I am going through shit. That's how bad I get to feeling. And now I have him on the back of my mind. I gotta make it through. I gotta make it through.*

[Wim] Cuyvers' grave for his father (1993) consists of two slabs of white stone of different sizes but with the same proportions, arranged like bed and pillow. Between the two slabs, a sheet of glass has been inserted vertically. This was to enable the architect's children to maintain the illusion that they could peer into the glass and see their grandfather's body, "To arouse their desire to look at death. To show death." His "Coffin for Donald Judd" (1994–5) is a prospective retrospective addition to the works of the sculptor, the one piece which Judd seemed to have failed to design. Using details, techniques and proportions lifted from Judd's work, Cuyvers designed a timber coffin. The idea of seeing the deceased through glass reappears here in the form of a fully glass lid to the coffin and is compounded by a hole through which the smell of the decaying body is able to escape, allowing the viewer to smell the presence of death as well as to see it.

—Edwin Heathcote, *Monument Builders:*
Modern Architecture and Death, Academy Editions, 1999
(NA 6148 H43 1999, University of Arizona Library of Art)

Dearly departed, we are gathered here today (or the day after, the day after the day after) to celebrate your departure, to acknowledge it and know it, to show it and smell it, to shake its heart, access its central ventricle, the hidden one be-tween the four, the hidden floor between floors four and five in the library that no one ever talks about, the decimal infinity opening to either side of every call number on every shelf. How to suggest the vast in glass? we ask. Maybe make a see-through theater in which all our asses are exposed. Seats below. Seats above. Seats in the future in which we might apprehend the past. By seeing through a thing to the end of vision can we understand our end? Our mothers are gone. Our fathers, they go on. How to comprehend that loss? we wonder. How to move past it as if an obstacle, stand under it for shelter from rain as if a promontory, walk out on it like the Hualapai reservation's U-shaped all-glass cantilevered Grand Canyon Skywalk on which you can walk out on a simulated nothingness, as close as most of us will ever get to levitation, either a glory of engineering or an eyesore on a treasure, and ask what it must have been like for them?

A letter can be an edifice. My mother's to me, when she knew that she would die, and soon, it's hardly bearable to think or speak about three decades later. Language, a monument. Our memories, monuments, unceasing, unspeaking. They go on forever until they, like everything, become ash. The space and air in the basement of this library suggest necropolis. There is no real-time conversation here: only this and what I find and leave in books. So many here are dead. What percentage of those on these shelves are gone? Gone in body? Gone in word? Gone from mind? Unchecked out for decades now? Someone must know.

Throughout history libraries have testified to what a civilization meant, or wanted to believe it meant. For now these codices will continue to contain them, at least in part, in the way we turn authors into myth, the way the essay creates a separate brain that can keep on Walter Benjamining after Benjamin is gone. Until the basement floods or burns, or the books are marked for discard and disposed of, how many lifetimes will be described in these pages? *Nuclear Explosions and Their Effects; Targets, Backgrounds, and Discrimination—Infrared Information Symposia; Soviet Military Psychiatry; Institute of Navigation Journal; Transportation Facilities; Detection and Remediation Technologies for Mines and Minelike Targets III; Hovering Craft and Hydrofoil,* the "First Hovering Craft & Hydrofoil Monthly in the World," including an Application for Membership form for the International Hydrofoil Society in which you're asked to name your Connection with Hydrofoils and Professional Qualifications, if any, signed Baron Hanns von Schertel, President, 1961.

Well, Mr. Hanns, I recognize the silent hours I spend among the stacks speak more of my own inwardness and predilections than the institution's failing star. The fact of my ass in this intentionally uncomfortable chair fingering these books suggests the library's living use, that this space, if filled by the dead, feeds the living, those passed needing less from us than we from them. What I want is to pry the heart out of the world and leave it flattened here, page 141. I won't get there, sure. We never were able to understand ourselves until it was too late.

Memorial Day, 2012

u·ncial, a. Obs.—° [ad. late L. sep-
f. L. sept-em seven + uncia OUNCE¹.]
UNT Glossogr., Septuncial, of seven ounces, or
of the whole.

or (se·ptiūр̄ı). [a. F. septuor, f. L. sep-
quatuor quartett.] = SEPTET.
CF. Life (1891) II. 177 The first and longest a
.the last a Septuor, very beautiful. 1873 'OUIRA'
.III Phrase after phrase, chorus on chorus, solo
r, and recitative.

ple (se·ptiup'l), a. and sb. [ad. late L.
, f. septem seven : see -PLE.] A. adj.
Ifold.
's Mag. I. 456 The 'quadruple' alliance will very
. 'septuple' one. 1868 LOCKYER Guillemin's
d. 3) 350, θ Orionis is a septuple star. 1882-3
Herzog's Encycl. Relig. Knowl. I. 49 The sep-
s of the Holy Spirit.
Having seven beats in a bar.
e's Dict. Mus. IV. 120/1 There seems no reason
poser, visited by an inspiration in that direction,

chre ; pl. the church of this order. Cf. SEPULCHRINE.
1844 A. P. DE LISLE in E. Purcell Life (1900) I. 130 Mr. and
Mrs. Craven met us at Mass at the Sepulchran Nuns. 1857
G. OLIVER Coll. Cath. Relig. Cornw. 30 The English Sepulchran nuns had determined to emigrate from Liege.

Sepulchre (se·pĭlkəɪ), sb. Forms : 2-7
sepulcre, 4 sepulchur, 5 scepulcur, sepulkyr,
5-6 sepulcur(e, sepulker, 6 sepulcor, sepulcar,
sepulcer, sepullcre, sepullcur, (sepulchree,
sepulchrie, sepulcrye), 6-9 (now U.S.) sepulcher, 3- sepulchre. [a. OF. sepulcre (11th c. in
Hatz.-Darm.), ad. L. sepulcrum (less correctly
sepulchrum), f. root of L. sepul-tus, pa. pple. of
sepelire to bury ; cf. Sp., Pg. sepulcro, It. sepolcro.]
1. A tomb or burial-place, a building, vault, or
excavation, made for the interment of a human
body. Now only rhetorical or Hist.
c 1200 Trin. Coll. Hom. 101 Oðer is þat bitwenen his
browenge and his ariste he lai on his sepulcre. a 1225 Ancr.
R. 170 Uor ʒe beoð mid Iesu Criste bitund ase ine sepul-

—*The Compact Edition of the Oxford English Dictionary*
Oxford University Press, 1971 (personal library)

Sepulcher. Alabamian. Kennel. Papeete. Retaliate. Like all words, these are doors
to open up new corridors, leading to another dozen doors, then each leads back
into the labyrinth, a familiar wind through books and stone. I've been caught in
ruts like this, in stacks like this, among the casks, the tuns, the old amontillados,
underneath the clockwork and the slow work of hearts a floor or two above us,
still broadcasting/telltaling from the past. Some words have freight, are freight—
when pressed they spring back, retaliate, they bring a fright, bring fight to nights
otherwise loose with dreams. You roll over in the bed; I am still awake. The
crosswalk sound from a mile away propagates through nighttime air and open
door: *walk, walk, walk, walk, walk, walk, wait.*

If the stacks collapsed, would we be entombed here in this library together, you
and I, pressed flat by dictionaries that are no longer current, to the extent any
dictionary was ever current (these things are not electricities: they just describe
how power works, how we used to say it worked)? Isn't this book just an echo
of the past, receding, echo, acceding to distance, pebble down an empty well,
an overheard moan in the library stairwell a floor above—descriptive of a love
affair or something over? Who knows how far away it was from us when we
finally picked its frequency up, given interval of starlight light and great distance,
Doppler effect and parallax, nerve delay and lag in comprehension, rendering
everything finally salient just on the other side of now?

You found me or I found you or somehow we found each other. Some nights this library echoes like a tomb. Other nights: a bomb ticks a floor below, waiting to shrapnel out your heart. Other nights: a kennel. The sounds of dogs. I have things to say about Alabamians, though I can't count myself among them, having only lived there for four years. Mostly I remember people saying *bless your heart* to me, only realizing a year later (another dictionary echo, that lag in understanding) that this was not meant as compliment but as blessing, offered on the heart of the deranged, profane, foolish, strange, disabled, or touched, so as to prevent damnation and confer protection. When spoken, some words confer protection: these are spells. Learn to spell them well and mind what they say of you.

Alabama, sepulcher of a state, houses revenants of warlost dead. At night they fight their war against the waking world again. Everything is overgrown, blown-up, and over: the kudzu creeping into the tornadoed swath; the Bellefonte Nuclear Generating Station mostly built but sitting idle in Hollywood, Alabama, still owned by the TVA; the lake left when the Martin Dam erased the town of Irma. So I imagined history like this, submerged like *Waterworld,* and skimmed the surface thinking *water moccasin* but never dipped a toe or thought of the forgotten dead. You hear stories. You read stories, *Deliverance,* for instance, and wonder about the darkened wooded spots that cameras and sentences rarely see. These too are echoes, in which we might hear our fears and confront them there. Look long enough to find the order in the orderless, conscious in the subconscious, waking life in dream, in dictionaries that network language between generations.

These books say: here's what we thought before, as recently as 1971. The *OED* omits place-names like *Papeete,* on another island I will never visit, named for a basket designed to carry water. Reader, put all your water in a basket. Note where it leaks out, and when. We call those leaks a tell, a frozen sea or margarita waiting for an ax to open it, maybe a martini in Tahiti surrounded by bikinis, thinking of another blown-up atoll a century of nuclear decay away. This is another echo, meaning single heart as solo moan. When I'm at home I think *away;* when away I think of home.

Surely it is obvious that this generation desperately needs silence and solitude. Life can be utterly transformed by quietness.

—Kirby Page, *Living Creatively*, Farrar & Rinehart, 1932
(HM 216.P3 1932 mn)

Note the date. We've always been concerned with the younger generation's needs. You too, bleached-blond forty-something DWF reading DFW in a major Texas airport, with fake boobs and too-tight tank. What are your needs? Is he meeting them, even as he could not meet his own? What are mine? Keep them in mind if you can. This will aid communication.

This note, this page, this spread, this book: it is an open line. I will always be here. If you are here, you too will always be, until we're not. If we're still ourselves, if we still ourselves for long enough, then we will fill and start to burst.

When I was twenty-three I spent a summer in silence. I knew no one in Ames, Iowa, weird little prairie heart to which I moved, so unless I used my hacked Radio Shack autodialer to steal long distance from a pay phone to talk to girls, I wouldn't speak until I went to shop after midnight in the twenty-four-hour Walmart. Gaunt and a little gnarly, I graced the place, hair spiked with inattention, those hours in aisles with the other zombies. We were all so well lit and creepy. We spoke to no one, and definitely not each other. Avoidance is why you shop at night. Porphyria, too, but that is far more rare.

You wouldn't call it a conversation, what we had, our moment, an exchange with the teller, but they know and use your name thanks to CHANT, Customers Have a Name Too, a Walmart policy in which the teller is instructed to address the customer by name if they show ID or use a check or credit card. Anything you can do to make the impersonal feel personal helps, they told me. I worked in another Walmart years before. The walls were oiled. The floor was waxed. Everything moved in tandem and efficiently when you did not look at it. The corrugated boxes stacked and packed flat for easier disposal or reusal. I wish I could say that my refusal to participate in the Walmart cheer we'd open the store with every morning got me fired, but that's not true. I cheered along with them. "Who's Number One?" "The Customer Is, Always!" "No, What Store Is Number One?" "2192, Houghton, Michigan! Whoop Whoop Whoop!" These words retain only a little meaning. The managers wanted our hearts, our conversion. A perverted belief in the power of the Mart of Wal, the punch clock on the wall, a genuflection at the smiley face on the floor on the way to break. Or at least you had to ape it, fake it, make it up.

Later in his book, Page writes, "Successively for ten days the regular reader will by vivid passages be stimulated to relieve human misery, to transform unjust social systems, to gain vision and serenity through silence, to explore great biographies, to follow the noblest personality, to run risks and accept penalties, and so on through the list."

I hope you live in silence by choice and not default. This is a mediated space. I am stimulating you to relieve your human misery or possibly my own. Is it okay if I finger a fold of your brain for a sentence length, for an essay length? Its curl and squishy ridge is warm, the consistency of butter (it's 10 percent fat, studies show), if not concussed.

I could confess anything here to you, knowing as I do that our connection is a long, thin strand. If you are here, in these Kirby Page pages, then you hope to live more creatively. I am living creatively. I hope you will do the same. Write me here. Write someone here. Write yourself into being here. I mean here you should write yourself into being. We are not who we are until we write ourselves and come to life.

This letter will have found you out in time. You will find me here in time. I will wait right here for your reply. I do not know your name, but I would like to.

DEAR SOVIET

(The Museum of Genocide Victims Library, Vilnius, Lithuania)

There's something Soviet about the wreck of Lithuania. See it in erasure of the former architecture, white plaster covering old detail, erection of identical Brutalist apartment towers in the distance. You occupied the country from roughly 1944 to 1990. Since then its capital—Vilnius—has rebounded, found its heart tuned toward the west, filled itself with cheeseburgers, pizza, Coffee Inns, free Wi-Fi, the Fluxus Bridge, subversive and playful art. In 2012 you can visit the Museum of Genocide Victims, formerly the KGB Museum, formerly the KGB prison and base of operations, actual site of the panopticon from which you—or those who held you down: I don't know how much you participated in oppression, whether or how much we can be judged for our dictators' actions—watched the city and its citizens.

In the prison basement of the building, though officially forbidden, it's not hard to take my picture in the cells, though not the isolation room or the water torture room, which can be peeked into but not entered. Then, entering the execution chamber, I walk on sheets of glass. Below me are possessions of the dead, or simulated ones: a shoe, some bones. Bullets, if we can call the causes of our death *possessions*. A burned page. Do we possess our own bones? I suppose. Until we don't. It's bright. A video loops on the wall and reenacts some horrors. I wonder about what's reconstructed, and from what.

You won't be allowed into the prison library, even though it's still filled with books. Barred, it barely merits mention on the signage. According to the Genocide and Resistance Research Center of Lithuania's Memorial Department, "Though prison records show that there were about 500 books there in 1950, the people locked up that year do not remember ever borrowing any books from it." One wonders what was there, then? Texts officially approved, vetted thinking, Communist propaganda? The answer's vague. "Only during the Khrushchev thaw, after Stalin's death . . . it was possible to order a book which was carefully checked before and after reading it (pages were counted, etc.). Only the prisoners who had the investigator's issued permission were able to use the library."

All stories are written on, over, or inside others' stories. In our moment here you and I might try to make up a we; that we might try to understand this interaction, the desire for new narrative (the one presented today is primarily of heroic, fierce Lithuanian resistance to decades of brutal Soviet repression and extermination; hardly mentioned are the ways in which empire was transferred after the Nazi occupation; only one small room mentions the Holocaust or the 190,000 Jews murdered here by Nazis and their Lithuanian collaborators), overwritten on the old. What does it mean to say *genocide* here? we wonder.

Some self-wreck, and some are wrecked by others; some dive the wreck to reconstruct; some build anew; some memorialize and monument; some photograph; some write on walls; some fill pages; some erase. It is not possible to know every story, or to unearth them, to know that they are true when we are told, to listen, or even to remember them once unearthed, palimpsest after palimpsest.

Since the photograph's not much, maybe it's enough to describe the scene: a wooden table, two feet by four, flanked by two seven-foot-high sets of shelves. Three green stools. Two short stacks of papers on the table that look blank. You can't see what's on the papers. One is yellow, one is pink. A place for notes, perhaps. But why? The window that does not open allows a little light, unlike the isolation cells. From the tiny access point, you can't make out the titles on the shelves, even if you can read Cyrillic. A small radiator in a depression. A vaulted ceiling, reminiscent of burned and then rebuilt cathedrals. It's not true that the wooden floors smelled of blood, silence, or starving brain, but it's hard not to think it here. What terror might you have felt during the occupation, the stacking of human horror on top of human horror, so that you forgot the latter in honoring the former. How were you complicit? How am I complicit in my seeing, in my being here? What story will you—will I—tell of our visit here? And what stories remain untold?

DEAR SPHERE

As for the library, the regulations that had to be followed were singularly severe. Books could not be taken out of the factory under any circumstances; they could be consulted only with the consent of the librarian, Signorina Paglietta. Underlining a word, or just making a mark with pen or pencil, was a very serious offense: Paglietta was expected to check every book, page by page, when returned, and if she found a mark, the book had to be destroyed and replaced at the expense of the culprit. It was forbidden even to leave between the sheets a bookmark, or turn down the corner of a page: "someone" could have drawn clues from this about the factory's interests and activities—in short, violate its secret.

—Primo Levi, *The Periodic Table*

Every library has its secret, sometimes more than one. What is housed among its stacks? What axis does this collection revolve around? Whose personality can be defined by the frozen brains that it contains? What keeps it whole, contained? Consider the library of the Biosphere 2, itself a library of plants, microorganisms, atmosphere, animals, insects, gases, and eight humans—not, during its first two-year run, one that lent or acquired (famously it was self-contained and self-sustaining, until it no longer was). Sixty-eight steps above the entry floor, the library tower still remains—but emptied of books. Eight bookshelves line the walls in the geodesic dome that rises high above the biomes below. The only part of the complex as high as the surrounding Arizona ridges, this was where the Biospherians housed their books. Four chairs and two couches remain, upholstered with space-age peach and blue; like the skunk, they emit a stench when provoked. There are three reading lamps and an antenna system. Two thin filaments quadrisect the room at about the halfway point above the floor. I don't know why. The whole thing is white with aqua paneling. Eight windows offer ports into the world beyond.

The library was elevated so the Biospherians, confined inside for two years, could get a broader perspective on the experiment, could rise above it in body and therefore in mind. But in fact their days were overworked, consumed with the activity of growing food, managing the atmosphere, and keeping themselves sane and alive. They rarely ever made the climb, especially as their oxygen declined. The stairs leave me out of breath (and this is with full oxygen). It's unventilated up here, very hot and stale. I was warned to come before noon, and even on an overcast day when I arrive at ten I can only bear an hour before gratefully descending.

In a library an hour away I find *Biosphere 2: The Human Experiment*, the account of John Allen, the Biosphere's administrator and progenitor. The title page has been written on and erased. After firing up the resolution on my scanner and tinkering with contrast, I can make out what remains: "Biosphere 2 [ ] [cidity enclose]" and then the signal fades. In the same book's back, in the pocket where its punch card once resided, here's a checkout slip and a card catalog card for Ernest A. Kraus's *Pathways Back to the Community* (RC 576 K7), its only listed subject: "Mentally ill—Rehabilitation." I wonder if it's just happenstance or if this finding's meant as a joke or if I should understand it as an oblique critique?

I had hoped to feel the Biospherians' presence here, to get a whiff of what it was to be so long contained (the longest voluntary isolation of humans on record), both patron and librarian, self-sufficient in every way, in 1991 and 1992. Instead I find just heat and light and stink, geometric loveliness, no trace of ghost or other haunting. No ideology or theory but that which the architecture promises and the baggage I brought inside with me.

DEAR SPHERE

(Library Tower, Biosphere 2, Oracle, Arizona)

The Biosphere 2 library tower no longer houses books. Instead, it houses light or the memories of books. Shelves of emptiness. The thought of work. Human absence, a little stinky. What remains of a grand, expansive, expensive dream. Books were here in 1991, removed, allegedly, by 1996 (though a report indicates that as late as 2001 you could still find some books here). There's no official record of what was on the shelves, but the space invokes infinity: see from here much of the Biosphere 2 and Biosphere 1, our globe it's meant to simulate. Stairs spiral down through a floor of glass to the main and basement levels where the offices are housed. Their curl suggests the whorl of conch, also present in the strangely heavy table inlaid with sediment and a seashell section at its center.

Downstairs in the kitchen, roped off from the tourists, a small stack remains on a counter. I let myself inside to check their spines. Here are Adelle Davis's *Let's Cook It Right;* a battered, unmarked *Joy of Cooking; Basic Microwaving, Revised Edition; SpeedCookers;* and *Cheese and Fermented Milk Foods,* second edition, books left by the Biospherians after their tour had elapsed and they could leave.

To haunt an empty library is to be surrounded by an absent history. What other books were here? I wonder. I imagine science fiction and ecology, novels set in outer space, on islands, or on boats, poetry to befit the space with metric stricture, maybe something inspirational to represent the administration's goals. Rebecca Reider answers, sort of, in her *Dreaming the Biosphere: The Theater of All Possibilities*, by far the best of the books about this expensive (and largely successful, contrary to its reputation) experiment: as of 2001, "an odd assortment of books still lines the shelves: collections of plays by great modern playwrights, ecology textbooks, legends of ancient civilizations, the Vedas, the Upanishads, literature on space colonies, how-to manuals such as *How to Grow More Vegetables Than You Ever Thought Possible on Less Land Than You Can Imagine*. Together, silently, the pile of books records a saga—a story of grand aspirations to understand and encapsulate the world. And tucked here and there amid all the books, other relics remain: a few slim volumes of play scripts from an acting company called the Theater of All Possibilities." I appreciate her report but still want more.

I venerate those of you who collect haphazardly and find your way to books erratically. You understand the pleasure in the happenstance, random encounter with a displacer beast in a simulated dungeon, the sort you used to lose yourself in for days in front of screens or in your parents' duplex with adolescent friends. From here memory multiplies into echoes. A continent and some years away Umberto Eco (or his Google alert, his assistant, his AI brain) overhears his name in conversation and responds, in his *The Infinity of Lists:* "There is, however, another mode of artistic representation, one where we do not know the boundaries of what we wish to portray, where we do not know how many things we are talking about and presume their number to be, if not infinite, then at least astronomically large." Therein we find sublime.

If a library is a message to the future, this one's mostly gone, only there in someone's memory, not mine. Now the only text that's here is on a fire extinguisher, or smeared labels on transmitters and antennas, and a torn note that reads:

STUDENTS:
please
Bio Ops
when you are
ready to go
back DownStairs.
Thx–

Squash—Advanced
Cucurbita pepo
Spaghetti Squash
Ss: Local
Pima County Public Library Seed Lending Library
Info: 791-4010
3 1152 06091 7657

Start this thought with a thing that is like another thing: *Cucurbita pepo,* spaghetti squash, filed under Advanced because of how hard it is to prevent cross-pollination, hybridization. It nauseates me to even write the word *squash,* so repellent do I find the plant. The reasons are what you'd expect: memories of barfing up the stringy mess, but before that the memory of being stuffed with squash and sugared up, pleasure before revulsion. Butternut, acorn, summer, table queen acorn, uchiki kuri, zeppelin delicata, pink banana jumbo, Pennsylvania Dutch crookneck, Magdalena big cheese, kabocha winter, green striped cushaw, galeux d'eysines, early prolific straightneck, buttercup, black beauty, baby bam pie pumpkin. Okay, the litany of names of seeds on offer here does cue my salivation, even though I wouldn't eat any of these varieties unless forced at point of gun or knife or beam from space or courtesy or God. Still, I love the variousness that the spread suggests—how rich our world, named, ordered, collected in a list.

Here in the Pima County Public Library's Seed Library at the Joel Valdez branch in downtown Tucson you can check out a pack of seeds to plant and grow. Six at a time at most for now. You do need a card. But there is no such thing as overdue for seeds: the library wipes them off your record after thirty days. Borrowers are asked to harvest seeds from a successful batch and "return" them when they can, assuming the seeds have not been accidentally hybridized. By this the library becomes a locus of literal growth, a catalyst for those whose hearts direct their hands on the soil and want to grow their world or food.

The collection here is a hedge against the future, genetic modification, the flattening of biodiversity into a thin, controllable, corporate, patented line. Not often have I found a place to be alive as this for the public good. All these seeds are heirloom, I'm informed. Each time I'm here, security—old dudes, exclusively, not armed except with pepper spray—keep walking by as if to check—for what, I wonder, packet theft? Other forms of unacceptable behavior? The code of conduct proscribes so many things: gambling, indecent exposure, harassing any-one, possession of whatever, shirtlessness and shoelessness, talking, of course, disciplining a child in an injurious or disruptive fashion, unsupervised children, sleeping, selling, lack of safety, "bringing into the library, or attempting to place or store in the library, bags, luggage, backpacks, boxes or other items larger than a surely arbitrary 17" x 22" x 15.5.""

The seeds are kept in card catalogs—remainder of the world before the Internet. You'll remember, if you're of a certain age, when you would slide open a wooden drawer and see the cards on either side of what you wanted, sometimes leading your search pleasantly astray. Products of human expertise, the work of hands and books and hours, the cards were composed of librarians' heirloom idiosyn-crasies. Now those are gone, cut into quarters to be used for scrap. What remains is digital, which shows no fingerprints. Convenient, certainly, and downloadable as an app, the online index lacks mystique and physicality. But that's the future we have made. Hard here, then, not to fetishize the past: the drawer's sliding-open sound, the packets riffling under fingers. Pick one and give it a good ma-raca shake: this is the sound of your future garden.

Dear squash, as noun or food or racket game you lack appeal. Though, almost onomatopoeia, you're a satisfying verb—sibilant, fibrous, quick and harsh, inte-rior made exterior by sudden pressure: you promise a gross explosion. You hold heirlooms, too, senses nearly lost: "the unripe pod of a pea. Also applied con-temptuously to persons," obsolete according to the *OED* for a hundred years or more, used a few times in Shakespeare. That too has been preserved, digitized. And now deployed. Planted here for you. A dozen seeds in a little envelope. Add water, grow in shade. Harvest when mature. Return your books.

> One July night he hit a fox with his Chevrolet and a
> particular string of bad luck followed. It happened outside

—Tom Chiarella, *Foley's Luck* (PS 3553 H448 f6 1992)

Three years after meeting you in Indiana, I thought of you again wandering through the *Esquire* website where your work sometimes resides. I admit it's not a magazine I often read (I'm uncomfortable reading *Esquire*—it's not sleazy exactly, but easy, aspirational, the way we can relax into our gender if we don't pay enough attention). I don't know how you feel about the magazine—I didn't ask—but you've worked there for some time, so it must be okay by you. It's okay by me too, though the sort of okay that's an oaky facade laid down on top of particle board on the sort of furniture I'm used to buying, frankly the only sort of furniture that you can find to buy these days, things not being what they used to be and all.

But here's the thing: I found your essay there, "The Art of the Handshake." I checked my skepticism—what did I need to know about shaking hands or the lives of men? There is some practical advice: "Think of the components: a swift, elegant movement toward the waiting hand, wise use of the eyes, the considered grip strength, even the rhythm of the shake." But then you take it somewhere else, more meditative and artful, unexpected. So I mean this letter as a kind of handshake—both with you and with whichever reader finds their way to you—this little bound corporeal you. Can an em dash be an ask, a handshake? If so, hello (a word bound to the telephone)—or hello reader, perhaps you came here, like me, seeking *Foley's Luck,* or perhaps you just happened on it (unheralded pleasure of the stacks; try that scrolling through your pdfs), liked the smell of the edition, were pleased by the type (Bembo, I note—a font I had an affair with), or got here from one of the related subjects noted in its library record ("Florida—Social life and customs—Fiction"—weird how these grace notes never function: if I wanted to read about the social life of Florida, how satisfying would I find *Foley's Luck?*). Regardless, dear Tom, it's good to meet you here again.

I've been thinking about deer, Tom. It's probably unrelated, how so far I've hit only one deer with my car, surprising given the density of nights spent driving in and out of the snowy, drunken, two-laned, deer-clogged heart of Upper Michigan (related subjects: animal death, bad luck, social customs, irony, belonging to a place, bad decisions, bad behavior, Mary Gaitskill, adolescence). This was in New Mexico, last year. I was driving a rented cop car prototype, a glorious Crown Victoria. It's an old-school car to rent: huge, bench seating, no iPod jack, no satellite radio; no CD player even—these beasts are not meant to convey in luxury exactly—but the tank hauls up hills. Driving back from a friend's wedding at which I officiated (he is Quaker, she is Pagan; the ceremony was a goulash; I wore a Moroccan robe with nothing under it and felt self-conscious for a while until I didn't; we performed Sappho courtesy of Anne Carson and jumped the broom) with my wife; we both were perhaps a little tipsy. There is a lot of dark in New Mexico. The road was straight and wide; there is a lot of high plain there too, though fewer drifters (they call them residents). Forty-five minutes still from Taos, where we were staying, I saw nothing (isn't that always the case) until suddenly: the deer—a big one, male; it was too fast to count the points—crashed into the Crown Vic's side. Bad luck, I suppose, or Foley's sort of it. I don't know how these things happen: what are the chances of a deer hitting a Crown Vic at what must have been full speed (I was at full speed myself)?

I didn't take it as a sign of anything. I pulled over up ahead. Of course I thought of that William Stafford poem. The car was untouched except for a touch of fur. The Vic's a beast. The beast itself I couldn't see; it must have run right back away, light reflecting off the surface of a lake. I'd like to think it was okay. I didn't hit it straightaway. Rather, it broadsided me. In this way we interfaced. Since it didn't even leave a dent (we'd hope our deaths would leave a dent), perhaps it lived, a little bent. I don't know enough about deer to say. Some nights you're in a car in New Mexico with your wife, and then the world becomes a bigger place.

Sometimes the letter starts before the epigraph: I wasn't sure where in *Foley's* to begin to write this card. I had your book in hand. I started writing, and took a swerve ("my only swerving") into my story of the deer. I read until I found the title story with carstruck fox and links of bad luck cascading through a life. A crux: whether to believe in fate (your Hank does, though it helps him not) or luck or deer aggression or invulnerability or masculinity, dirty martini with three olives, or should I address it in a letter (dear aggression), if anything like that can help us live.

—*Playboy* 45, no. 12 (Dec. 1998), Braille ed., part 1 of 4 parts (Tuscaloosa Public Library)

It's an easy joke to make, amusing contradiction, the Braille *Playboy*, holding it and trying to make a point about the book qua book: that the codex form isn't always as we think, that different books must serve different needs. Magazines, okay, not books, and there's the question of how to represent the airbrushed female flesh that defines the magazine (that flesh—itself a simulation, stand-in for real bodies we might once have believed we'd touch as we touched our own—is not included in Braille translation, only the articles and other text). So, stripped of whatever sex it had, I hold it here, and holding, see (a joke) the appeal of books in Braille, light like puffy paint printed on puffed rice, not the dense untextured pages that the slighted sighted use. Holding an artifact like this I know what I am missing: dreams of passing light, the feathered breath of paper, comprehension through touch, unceasing darkness that I don't know is darkness.

Those girls in those puffy-painted shirts: I don't want to say they haunt my dreams (they don't, or not exactly—the '80s style returned without my knowing, so recent days in malls are arrested by reminders of the past), but I wonder what light it might have made in my life to run my hands down their shirts, faces, pretending I was blind.

I get that writing this this way won't reach you either; I'm not just a chump for irony. Better would be translating it to Braille, etching it in skin with a stylus so you could feel it swelling up all along my book—my back I mean, these things with spines get entwined in brain; these corpora are so easily conflated when we lose ourselves in books—in time. When did I wonder what it would be like to live in a sightless world? When did I try it for a couple of hours? Dilettante, blindfolded, idiot trying to learn a world by wading in it, then I felt a fool, forgot it until just now.

So far I am untattooed, not just because of wussiness but for lack of an idea good enough to sear on flesh. I've got a commitment problem, and I'm not just talking about the increasingly unhinged activity of lonely, isolated relatives who collect delusions and cocoon themselves in snowy climes. Something must be done. Nothing can be done. That's called living, homes. The only thing I've ever thought enough to ink on me would be an image of an arm, and on that arm, a tattoo of an arm, until you could no longer see it in the density, but then the thought: too cute to be worth the pain? Too self-reflexive? Or else as many digits of pi as I can remember and stand. My wife's name. A heart, not the simplified kind but the bulbous ugly blood nexus that makes us go.

I've considered signing in to Shelley Jackson's *Skin,* a 2,095-word story in progress "published exclusively in tattoos" according to her FAQ. Check its progress here: http://ineradicablestain.com/skin.html. Weird to offer up a link that might well be down or gone or disappeared by the time this meets your eyes or hands or ears or heart, but it's the most honest way to direct your attention there. Like asscrack abutting lower back stamp reading "irony." What if I committed a URL to skin, a gateway to the cluttered paradise we thought the Internet would be. In WilliamGibsonWorld we'd all have dataports by now to allow the net to penetrate us physically.

I've been watching 1990s movies about the future of the world: virtuality, immersivity, and verisimilitude; then we felt that we could lose ourselves in bits. Now it seems a little quaint. We ain't got that far that fast, and the meat we walk around in continues to exert quite a bit of force: bodily desire, revulsion, the sunburn peel, hunger for Doritos, a memorable scent like sandalwood: these things are hard to shake. We'll never shake them, shackles. Even writing them I think of them. I suspect it'll be the same for books: if there's something in the artifact that connects to us and what is written there, then they're not / we're not just ghosts in shells, waiting to shed ourselves and become something else.

The task of perception entails pulverizing the world, but also one of spiritu-
alizing its dust.

—Gilles Deleuze, *The Fold*

This note's hope is manifest in this: that in reading and in writing letters halfway
to forever we can multiply ourselves, manifold of many folds, men with folded
cloaks, folds of many sheep, mini-foals made miniature of pewter, about a half-
inch high apiece, 1/10 scale, figurines for gaming use, in shearing dreams, in the
sort of dreams you share with a lover if you want to flatter them with the extent
of your strangeness. I hereby hope that we might publish ourselves into a future
ether, and so I am doing it. Dear silence, dear future, a future filled with deer
clotting Upper Michigan roads so deep you have to nudge them gently with your
car, or they won't and you won't move an inch. And this is before the par-
alyzing snow. Either the future will come or it will not. Either I will be there or
I will not. No way to know. At least I will be here, so if here is there—if all of
this is not discarded or eroded or otherwise destroyed—then I will be your guest
as ghost.

Dear disambiguation, will you keep this note or return it to its fold inside the
book? It's meant for you, your eyes, the strands of hair that sometimes shield
them from my own. I imagine you as girl, as object of desire. For me the future is
an object of desire. That desire—folded into multiplicities—propels me through
a paragraph, engines my eyes to the next. Imagining you with your hands upon
this book, my lines, turns on in me the longing mode, the dreaming mode, the
prestidigitation mode. Now I want to listen to Depeche Mode and get a good
mope going.

Quick trip to the wiki showers us with manifold options for our disambiguation: exhaust manifold or hydraulic; inlet; manifold chemistry; vacuum manifold; "an abstract mathematical space which, in a close-up view, resembles the
spaces described by Euclidean geometry"; England's River Manifold; Sir Walter
Manifold, 1849–1928; John Manifold, 1915–1985; "the third stomach of a rumi-
nant" (O. Goldsmith, 1774). The language splits and we might choose our own
adventure, pleasure of the wiki, pleasure of the referent, its many meanings, the
definitions doubling and doubling like a zygote, the minimeanings like those
ruminants that might fit inside another, as in penned, contained, religiously

maintained. A word can contain glossy multiplicities and does not have to be resolved. No word can contain the all of us—or even the fingerprint of our breath, a hint of curry still manifesting from last week. No mind or letter can contain your all, you know. Your awl, no man can contain your half, you understand. To perceive a thing is to crush it, make it miniature, tiny Minotaur in our micro-labyrinth of brain, the one we built ourselves, the one we hid our desires in to keep them safe, to keep us safe, to keep the world separate from the word, the straggler from the herd, the thought from what is overheard, then become the deed, the one we long for most and cannot have, the game of keep-away that electrifies the self. By this fence, these words, the West was penned. May you keep yourself away. May you fold this and take me with you in this way.

E

First of all—and this justifies the plain brevity of the title—what is the significance of e? Why should it crop up so often, even in such simple things as charging a capacitor from a constant voltage?

—M. G. Scroggie, "e," *Essays in Electronics: Some Further Thoughts by "Cathode Ray"* (TK 7827 S37 1963, Fresno State University Library)

Can't start with that, *'l*ctric curr*nt,* and no fair to work with stars standing in for a glyph, cuz it's as difficult to omit as anything you could think of in this lingua. To work without any is to work without a big ol' tool (so says a poor porn star). So: can't drill down in rock to grok its gist, can't talk simply of folio or print, can't go happily computing as I am wont to do, can't dynamo a photon or amass signification without mass awkwardity or violating my way of writing this.

So I'll start again. Avoiding it is my pathway to you. Though I don't know your body, brain, location, any of that data, I trust you'll grok my approach. I won't know you, probably, so you could apparition as anybody in this library without my noticing or saying so. You, a ghost in that black chair, black skirt, black tights, imagining slow lights tracing a glow around your body, mugging for any who might look: you know what it is to b (ZOMG!) commodity. Your anthropological script. Your bookish disposition. Or you, in that limp hat, oui, you: scanning microfilm with a magnifying, zooming apparatus. Or you, about to scrawl a horrid slur in that book's margin. What's going on in your indoors that you would commit this act? You, typing on your voltaic laptop apparatus, board of clacking, buzzing glyphs, imagining a hippogriff, a gryphon, hybrid anything to split this day in half and carry you away.

In a library you know by now it's hard to find your way around a word, a world. Any turns out to b a crux, a major cog. (I know I could go all txt or l33t sp33k on your ass but that's a bit limp.) To work around a blank's a plank walk out on top of a long drop to agua with barracuda. My brain is scrambling now, lighting up again in nova ways. This is what it is to go Oulipian. Drop just 1 of 26, but just don't think about it (isn't this civilization's trick, a walk across a void: don't think about animal us?) and I'm okay. You too, you two, dirty talking against that stack about your forthcoming assignation.

On my way out I might brush against y'all's coats or parasols as laid across your chairs, or catch a look at what you zoom too quickly through. What do you want to find on this bottom floor?

So many digital transmissions pass through my I in an instant. All that data. All this transitory information, all this crypto that I can't crack. As such am I I or am I us (or am I Roman digits in film copyrights, so many Ms and Cs and Xs anachronizing up my brain), an amalgam of thought and sound and light? Am I dispatch or am I its wrapping? Am I atomizing? Can I still call my I an I or am I a patchwork of all of our communication?

If I avoid, am I what I avoid? Your ghost is in a shadow I am casting from an indoor light all along your coat, your chair, your glossy hair. I am standing in your light, you say, unknown bookish sort. Sorry is what I say, and drift into an adjoining corridor in which I find a dozing youth, and cannot pass without a password or his waking. If I don't shift back, I'll block your light again and risk your irritation doubling as you work your way through a history of digital art in print. So who is haunting whom today? In Alabama you might dub a ghost a *haint*. So many haints in y'all's South, in stacks, in ruinlight.

If you got carstruck and your skull was split so as to find skylight and long strands of song uncurling—and you lost words for things such as *schwa* or *God* or *Broca's* spot—if you could train your brain again to pick up words to fit a world and in so doing claim it again as yours, with a slight shift, its axons might again conjoin and transmit spark in auxiliary ways: though this you might transform, contort, switch your way of calling out who and what and why, patch what gaps you find in I, and bring you back to a world of forms you don't know what to call.

```
591.92                                    3932
Rud
Rudloe, Jack.
   The erotic ocean.
```

DATE	ISSUED TO
7-21-77	Robert Austin
9-27-78	Sara W. Maryin
7-22-79	P ALLEN
	C Moll
1/28	HAYNES
Dec 30 81	K Spellman
7/15	B Maynes
4/25	CAgStiven
8/13	V Brown

GAYLORD 40

—*Specialists' Meeting on Systems and Methods for Aiding Nuclear Power Plant Operators During Normal and Abnormal Conditions,* Baltonaliga, Hungary, 4–6 October, 1983
(University of Arizona Science & Engineering Library)

I found the card, but not the book, stuck in the back of another book, either a placeholder for a reader or maybe just a spot to stash a card they kept in a bag for years, a reminder of a time they spent with a much-desired oceanographer contemplating the sea's infinity and then the body's after.

Please take your pick of infinities. Try God, for instance, or mathematics. June sun in Arizona, maybe, a closeness to the sun-blasted planet Mercury, if not the fleet-footed man of myth. Or snow's infinity, a never-ending Michigan rend of time and space in airborne ice, is also nice to think about when there is nothing else to do except think of it, what surrounds you this afternoon in your northern cabin as you settle into memory after memory. These are infinities too; you could follow them down forever into erotic reverie. Remembering memories re-encodes them chemically.

Now the book itself is gone—was it ever there? Not here at least: that it's coded Dewey tells me it originated in another library. "Maynes" was a two-time visitor, or else there were two Mayneses who checked it out, the wife before the husband, following on the trail of the other's suspected infidelity. Where might it have started, he wondered, the divergence of her private life from her public face, with a book, for instance, *The Erotic Ocean* surely a good candidate for this brand of wandering? In consulting her reading log he found his way to this. Where did it lead you, Maynes? Where did it lead you after, B. Maynes? Your heart's a maybe, as you always knew it was, as weak as you'd long feared but couldn't admit, the product of a convenient life. Did it lead you back together, your trawls down the labyrinths of another's reading life? Did you find your other's curious heart waiting for you there, as if all of this was just a test?

Every sentence is a corridor. It's easy enough to miss it if you don't pay enough attention. Walking down the Rillito River Park pathway in Tucson underneath the bridge at Campbell, you might note the tunnel off to the side, man-sized, vanishing into the earth. Not the sort of place you'd think about unless you were in a certain sort of mind, looking to wander away from your life and way of being in the world and into another. Thus this route underground goes nearly two miles into darkness, punctuated by traffic-on-manhole ring and the occasional animal clatter beyond your vision. What heart or words might be found there? This detour is an incision into another's skin, trying her—or him—on for an afternoon, a paragraph, a page, and just like this you might become one of the many other lives you imagine must be out there, just on the other side of consciousness. How can we ever understand another? We are so interior. A trace like this might guide us or lead us incompletely into darkness.

> A wet year in northern Arizona produces a large ring in the pine trees, and a
> dry year produces a small one.
>
> —A. E. Douglass, "Tree Ring Dates and Dating
> of Southwestern Prehistoric Ruins"

Are you listening, Denis Wood? I don't know if you wanted to be mapped to
Boylan Heights, but in my mind you have. Knowing it is knowing you, is knowing your obsession. I still don't know the feel of it, of course, having never run
its blocks, having never enumerated its trees and mapped them as you have. But
I know the way you've tried to understand it, to take it apart and put it back together: Boylan Heights, I say, and feel the wordsound in my mouth. Nothing
happens when I say it. When you say it, though, something happens. It opens
like a magic action. Splits itself apart into a dozen maps, then each of those, they
separate, and keep separating.

Where I am from is still largely unwritten. Zero for most of the world, it's a
one for the lucky few who know it. Full of it even in absentia, we know it well:
we know it's ours; we've made it so through hours of living in it, living through
it. Everything is underground or undersnow. Everything is trees and water and
diminishing summer. Everything is rings of trees and amateur radio waves blan-
keting everything, invisible, indivisible.

Everyone sings where I am from. The pain must take a shape. They shotgun the
signs where I am from. That's percussion, a way of singing, too. Robert Pinsky
says the medium of a poem is the body of the reader.

Everything's rings, a circle around where I'm from and where I am. We cannot
get away from from. You know. Where we're from is where we're from. We can
punch it down like rising bread but not shake its stink from us. From where we
are we might think it silly, strange, that place of origin, why would anyone live
there, fall in love there, fall in love with it? But what do we know? How can
we plot how it rewired us?

Every sentence is a ping where I am from, bit pulse sent to test a circuit, check to
see if someone or something's listening on the other end. The response could
be a year or a century from now, but still we make the call.

If you were to cut my life in half, you could read it by the rings it would contain. You contain them too: who you used to be is enclosed in who you are. Your old heart is not erased. It's encased in another heart, another axon-dendrite shell stacked, shellacked atop the old. We are a wasps' nest of selves, each embedded in the next.

It's okay to know. We can change our lives. Some of us do so dramatically; some unintentionally. Maybe we hit a guy walking across Speedway Boulevard, named the ugliest street in America by *Life* in 1970. Maybe it was dark; he was wearing dark colors; he was walking out, not in a crosswalk, occupied by a map. You were waking. And then the rubber marks tires leave on asphalt when they try to stop: they were left on you. They are still on you. What does it mean to say it was not your fault? Your old life is gone; it's covered by another—by the other's life you accidentally ended.

This is a real fear of mine. Tucson, Arizona—the place from which this note is composed—is built of cars and grid of streets. Someone's always getting hit. Maybe it's the heat. That's a map. I fear that either I will go this way—hit from behind, skull opened to the sky, hand trepanning it to lowercase the swelling—or I will hit someone with my car, map their heart along its hood. You might see the ring a year later, a decade later: skid mark, blood, concrete, broken spoke, and fault. Go get a malted milk. It'll help replace that mouth taste with another.

Everything's strung together like this: a read sentence suggests another. An essay leads us to a book, which contains a pair of hairs—one human, one pet—caught in a fold. As we know, each human hair contains a world of information and connection if we look closely enough. Hair connects us to the animal world, in which we are driven by urges from millennia ago: sex, safety, hunger, satiety. If hair contains the curls of DNA, then in it we are reproduced. We've mapped that, helpfully.

Everything swings, is singed, the burn circle out back beyond the barn in memory where my Estes model rocket set the whole field on fire and my cousin Jay had to be roused to put it out. Do you remember? he asks, when I see him. Yes, I say. I do. I thought the world would burn that day and would be replaced by another, darker one.

This colophon serves as a certificate of authenticity. It is issued by Lisa Pearson, publisher, Siglio Press, Los Angeles, California, and is signed and numbered by the author and mapmaker Denis Wood.

—Denis Wood, *Everything Sings,* limited edition (Rare Books Collection, University of Arizona Poetry Center Library, copy 2)

Everything's signed by brain or hand or heart, Denis Wood. That signing is a map. Your hands were on this edition, in a room somewhere, your Boylan Heights perhaps, or in Los Angeles. In the age of disassociation and fragmentation, history-free ebooks torrented on the Internet, burger meat from random cows gathered up in drive-thru fast-food burger patties to be liked, live-tweeted as we eat, there's also this: a thing, an artifact, complete with Hancock and finger trace, which makes it more than other books, we're meant to know.

Reading anything is a risk, rare books more so. This might take me over if I let it, if I open myself up to it. Left alone, I feel a double nervousness, an electricity, like I'm bound to slash. I want to fuck it up somehow, fracture this life from the one before my error.

In Colorado I hear about the fires. Everything is singed there, I think, dinged with particles of smoke or fear of smoke, or thoughts about what smoke might mean if inhaled, if it spread toward the bodies of those we love who still live there. I wonder if Boylan Heights has ever burned. In my own Upper Michigan this summer was marked by fire. It was wet when I was there, but just a week before, it burned. The Seney Stretch, straight and long throat of road, often obscured by blowing snow in winter: driving it you see spaces opened up by blaze now just filling in with new.

Aficionados of prairie fire in western Illinois understand that only in flame can new growth come. Sometimes one must burn a thing to make it live: it's not enough to build it up, to rehab and refurbish; instead it must be reduced to ash.

I'd love to torch your book and see what would come out. Would the pages curl and reveal a new map of Boylan Heights in char, or someplace else beneath it? Would the vellum maps of the limited edition, backlit for a moment before they conflagrated, align and open up the world? Oh, I recognize it's just a book. It has no secret name, no special powers. It's not the magic I once wanted hard to believe in. It's not sodium chunks liberated from the chem lab dropped in toilets at the high school just to hear the boom. It's not the towering flame of the stairwell sawdust column, scattered from four floors above and descending, lit from the bottom and burning all the oxygen that forced the school's evacuation.

I admit that was a bad idea. Collect enough of them and you can map my life this way. Maybe it's worth it just to have seen a thing like that, as if by force of thought and action we transformed an afternoon of school into a memory that still sings these decades later. That is a map of something, map to something, map to my former self, perhaps, and its weakness for vandalism. We signed that place in fire, or dreamed we did. And now it's gone except in memory, the high school moved, and what we thought we knew decayed.

Your maps sear the eye because they essay: they show—they are—a brain operating on the world. Through them we experience place—but also self as it sees a place. They venerate the I through the action of the eye. Boylan Heights is singed by you, what you saw there, what you made of it; it's signed by you, and that's what keeps us here with your inventions, your associations. Thus my Boylan Heights is bent beneath your Boylan Heights, and I'm happier for the pressure and attention, more aware of the constellation of jack-o'-lanterns on my paper route along my own Woodland Road, age thirteen, before I moved away.

Pank the world into a flattened transposition, which is what we do in the North to snow: we can't get rid of it, you understand; we move it, or failing that, we pank it down with shovels into a flattened path that we might traverse with dogs or sleds, snowshoes, skis, stories, maps like this, memories of hearts, or other powerful machines.

A labyrinth is said, etymologically, to be multiple because it contains many folds. The multiple is not only what has many parts but also what is folded in many ways. A labyrinth corresponds exactly to each level: the continuous labyrinth in matter and its parts, the labyrinth of freedom in the soul and its predicates.

—Gilles Deleuze, *The Fold*

I'm not sure a labyrinth is multiple. The proper labyrinth, to use the current derivation, is unicursal: it has but one path to follow, though it bends. Hence the split of *maze* from *labyrinth:* mazes are multicursal, with dead ends and forks. A maze is made to lose you, get you lost. You can lose yourself in a labyrinth.

Two hairs caught in this book's spine bring it to life. One is probably a pet's. The other's human. Beard or something nether? It's reddish, little, curled inward, secreted away in the gutter as the pages fold into the signature and are there stitched. Must I remind you that you have a body, reader? You are not just a brain even if you read Deleuze. I like to imagine you nude with Deleuze, still life, pet on a lap around the room, considering your lap, now occupied with book. *Reading is sexy* reads the shirt I wear sometimes, and it is.

In this way you, former reader from whom I just recalled this text—a jarring reminder that there are others who also read, and read Deleuze, and are connected by desire: we both want & want this book—you and I are paired. Your hair here. I tucked in one of my own. Then are we one, just flipped and opened up?

You and I are connected at this point, the point exactly of our brains in this moment sharing this sentence, this breaking of silence, this semiautomatic fan rattle hum. You are I, in this trench of I this rut of broken thought, such as it is, I made. The sentence is both silence and separation from it—unspoken unless you are speaking it, stitching your voice to mine, your locus voci with my own.

The world has so many foci to consider, scattered everywhere on the ocean floor. Pick one up as you are moved to; now consider it, beach-washed conch, ring your world around it for a frozen moment, a silent omen, fold everything into it, those lovethoughts from a year ago, the frozen lemon slushy. Get lucky in this way exactly: anything folded back upon a point will echo that point, pair with it.

Pare it all away if you can. This is what white space does: contains an echo, screens—as in a scrim—the page behind.

The brain is folded too. One thought pressed in on another, often without intention. A partial memory of a breast (perhaps your own) superimposed on some hours spent playing *Sentinel Worlds 1: Future Magic.* A cruel word, a gruel of world, a drooling bird, your cat's strange conversation with the sound of packing tape as it considers plucking that bird from the air and vivisecting it. Bruce Weigl tells me something else from a dozen years ago in verse. I don't know if I can trust him, if he'll truss me up, dump me in the darkened water with a Christopher Davis poem, an old one like "Jojo's" or "The Killer," in which I might best be thought of as a blood and bubble trail through the water until you lose sight of me and the vector of my descent so that I am untraceable at last.

A pencil lead leaves a rut, not just a dark mark, as it moves over and into a sheet of paper, which is why it cannot be completely effaced. We leave marks all along each other as we pass and pair and disconnect in discotheques. I fear it's what we're for.

To perceive may be to receive, to oculate, to orb, to parse, to grok, to understand if there is—or to create—a pattern in it, Larry Levis, the plot against the giant, Susan Howe, or other Howes, operating on ice like Gordie. To iterate a thing is to make a fold in language, to damage or construct by duplication, knowing then that this thing must exist again in another couple dozen pages, a few punctuation marks away, a breath a break, a day away. To fold a text, to couple up a pair of words around whatever point, to copulate a world or worlds into being, to compile a worm from segments, to reconstruct a body from memory, to be so bold, in a moment like this one, is to become.

The neighborhood: a metabolic machine

—Denis Wood, *Everything Sings*

IN AN ATTEMPT TO REACH YOU AGAIN

—e-mail message from "A. M. Garcia," informing me
of my dubious $25.5 million bequest

Dear Denis Wood, after reading you, this year I've come to know the extent of
the Tucson storm sewer system, the tunnels singing, pinging, underpinning the
upper world. I want to know the western sprawling city grid anew: so I follow
where all the water goes when it monsoons. In August as I write this there is
rainpound everywhere: the blank of air is filled with gush; streets flood and drain
into the washes, gulches, arroyos, where they rush into the Rillito River, which
winds into the Santa Cruz, and disappears north. Roads become impassable; a
bridge erodes; the city is reversed.

You come to know a layer of a place when you are there so long you forget what
it was like above, when your senses adjust to what the tunnels offer: graffiti spray
and bits of flotsam, trashed glass, traffic manhole cover clang, twists of wire on
walls, the occasional insect scuttle sound, and, when raining, wet infinity.

Paint marks on walls make up a map of how far in you went, who was here and
when, who fucked whom, who loved whom, and when, until they didn't any-
more. Who lied. Who died. Who rulez the skoolz; who adornz the Zs with a
diztinctive zpray paint trail. These notes belong to the lonely, the homeless, and
the young: who else finds their way into these secondary spaces?

Less than an hour away, you miners who plunder copper from the mountains
south of Tucson: How do you understand the world beneath this world? Is it
more than an economy to you?

A century and 1,564 miles away, you Finnish miners who cut a living from
the Copper Country of my childhood, on the border of Superior that borders
Canada: What did you know, working your lives in the underneath? What was

your world like without the sky for days, buying your own candles, contemplating the threat of gas or roof collapse or filling lungs, knowing that your need for light and a living had a cost?

Or you bored, gorgeous preening teens who broke the locks on the long-closed doors and explored the shafts with spray paint, beer, and radio, wanting something else from your isolated lives: what respite did that darkness offer you?

I think of light 5,899 miles away, in Vilnius, Lithuania, a city in which I rarely hear my language spoken. The library in which I work is dark, five centuries old and counting. Everything is ornate wood, made to be admired, not used. My laptop's on the huge reading table surrounded by banker's lamps, glass-encased Mercator maps, and books of exploration, a display of desiccated spices brought back from places exotic, east. Cinnamon and garlic, coffee, chocolate, cardamom, vanilla: the desire for these once drove (or financed) our explorations into the other, the open spaces on the map. What must it have been like to make your way away from known and into the uncharted?

I know I'm drawing circles here, charting pairs, but isn't that what a map is for, corresponding thing with thing: that ridge; that colossal palm; the tallest, oldest pine in view; the spill of porchlight light on golden hair; a flash of underwear; a Rorschach blot; a dying wish; a dish-filled sink; the shortwave radio you could hear from there and there alone; oil stain in a driveway; a border of a country; a hazy patch of memory?

In 1977 the Office of Charles and Ray Eames produced a short film, *Powers of Ten*, in which, starting from far out in space (scale of 10^{24} meters), the camera zooms in an order of magnitude each two seconds on the center of the previous frame, to Earth of course, a couple picnicking just off Lake Shore Drive in a Chicago October, then inside the man's hand, his skin, deep in the cellular interior, ending (in the film version; subsequent books pushed in farther) in the center of a proton of a carbon atom. Much is known, we see, but more is not: On either end, the micro and the macro hold infinities. What is outside us? What is inside us? What is under us? What does the heart hold? What of the dark-adjusted eye? What of the brain, forever voyaging, making maps of what we know and don't?

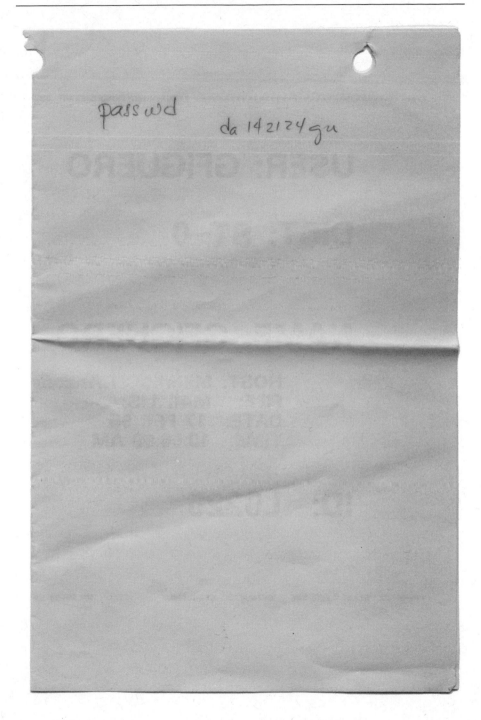

passwd

da 142124 gu

—D. H. Rawcliffe, *Illusions and Delusions of the Supernatural and the Occult*
(The Psychology of the Occult), Dover Publications, 1959 (BF 1031.R3 1959)

Found inside: an envelope, or a photo of one, or a sort of photorealistic drawing of one, white on a black card, covered by a gritty dust, and hard not to think
a specter evanescing from the book, a sort of joke, one thinks, investigations of
the occult tough to take seriously except that statistics show more than half of
Americans believe there are things beyond what we can see and touch: angels, for
instance; demons, ghosts. Waking fears include the haunt of terrorism or infidelity, or our children taken without trace while we were sexting our sexy exes, how
we failed as parents as evident as anything on our faces, and the dreamlike litany
of the things we could have done, the ways we might have paid more attention,
fixing our lives around their stars, immobile until the gravity's gone. Also the
spells of drugs, elision of waking life and dream, online predators or exes found

on Facebook after decades of embedded, superpowered fantasy. Photographs of axes gleaming along barn walls in rural Michigan, evidence of hard work or else cultists, pervasive satanic ritual from the 1980s. The nuclear melt: our faces sloughing off in dreams. The labrys, the double-bladed ax that lends its name to the labyrinth where we bury what's most important to us. The ghosts we fuck and are fucked by at night when we leave our consciousnesses at the door. Whatever's hidden in the basement, the casement window sound wound through the empty home on windy nights is evidence enough of what's beyond, killers, maybe, rapists, or the sublime, or both, and god we know there must be field beyond field after this, something must come after this, because this cannot be all, and if we wait and nothing does, if all our demon dreams are random chemical fire filtered through the sieve of brain that must make meaning out of everything, then what?

Even now we try to chide it, shut it off, the fear of nothingness, the fear of some-thingness, bad habits, blood trails on snow into the winter carnival maze where the girl was killed, we fail so slowly in this way: into the boring dreams of our common age, to be so typical, the limited range of sexual fantasies and frustrations or, worse, the loss of those drives into slowly draining swimming pools our teenage daughters tan themselves alongside, gorgeously courting cancer, and it's hard not to fear them too, those girls, ourselves, bearing drawings of envelopes addressed to us and sent from the beyond. Inside are the secret things we punch down below memory, those we failed and how, our wailings, where the trails led in our childhood yards, our wallings-off, the screens we throw up in front of the world to keep it off our lawns, away from our homes, the bodies buried there, the warm skulls of guns we keep in closets for protection, the illusion of control. Something's peeking through the eyehole now, it always is, pressing outward on the fabric of what we perceive like a face in muslin, Muslims all eyes and anger in those clothes we're sure, the ineffable other speaking to our well-groomed girls on Ouija boards, saying something inadmissible about atomic light, birdflight, the end of empires, our desires.

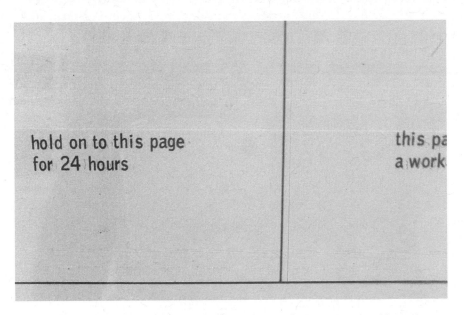

—Ben Vautier, "Fifty-eight Propositions for One Page," *Fluxus Newspaper No. 7,* 1965
(Fluxus Cabinet, Contemporary Art Museum, Vilnius, Lithuania)

Then you may release it where you will. I suggest a fold, then place it in a book or on a wall. Listen to the bell song tolling from the church until it's over. Hooked tourists may find it here in a dozen years or maybe more. Do your part. Speaking to the future is an art, ongoing. How do we remainder our days into memory? Will the thousand photographs you took of every angle of every battlement of every castle bring to life this day you spent wandering a city with the one you love? Some days I'm not sure what memory is worth. Twenty-four hours is a day, a way of tracing time. Spend it without speaking. Your thinking will be worth these silent hours. It'll build itself into a mound of dirt. Plant something in it this time tomorrow. Hold your silence. Fill the remainder of this page with your thinking, then your speaking. Writing is slow speaking. Reading is fast thinking. If you are unused to silence, give it time to root. Have patience, nations of the world, represented by these shambling, ambling groups of tourists mumbling to themselves in their strange languages. These may not present your face the best to us, just as I do not mean to represent America fuck yeah, the colonial, the imperial, the impervious, the permeable, yet I suppose I do regardless: I am a library for these dreams. Let these monuments consume you. There are so many and they are so old. That much time is hard to hold. So don't. Start with a day. A page. A stage for making something. This side is mine. The next is yours to fill with what you have to say. Give yourself this day to give yourself away.

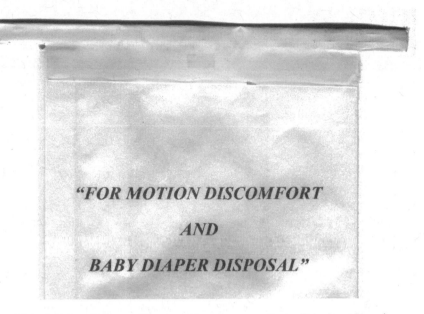

"*FOR MOTION DISCOMFORT*

AND

BABY DIAPER DISPOSAL"

(United Airlines flight 5437, Tucson to Denver, 5:15 a.m., Seat 10D backseat library)

Not for lending, these volumes, *SkyWest* magazine, with a feature on "Michigan: Keweenaw Peninsula," my home whether or not I'd like to claim it. These things claim us: the winter crush, the lack of touch for weeks, a conversationless month so silent that one late night I sojourned, unintentional monk, to the Walmart just to catch a human voice. It fell away soon enough, brief drift from the cashier's midnight mouth to the fluorescent hum, then my Chinese junk stowed safely in the car in dolphin-throttling plastic sacks, as if the night had meant to say this long silence is a sentence diagrammed for you and you alone.

This library is small, meant for me alone, the collection limited. The CRJ700 Passenger Safety card, there to stay, beside the point, as we all know, since all we'll be is teeth and Great Lake vapor—name of a new smokeless cigarette— when we go down in flame and last question death mask, but we kowtow to ritual, pretend to pay attention, just like in school. We got good at that, the darkening, the silence, tuning out this world, tuning into another, like cracking an egg and finding in its place another egg but this one filled with glowing something special, and worthy of our hallowed study, our days counting down in study hall to the end of winter.

I study *Hemispheres* from Continental Airlines, crossword only partly done, of course. Number 37 across, "a book of maps," five letters—they got this one, "atlas," and this mag is too an atlas: here's where we fly, you and Continental Airlines and possibly the hand of god, the clean circular routes to suggest dimension. But for 91, three letters, "forest female," I think they must mean elf, but that's crap as any reader knows: elves can too be male or perhaps like always I am up the wrong tree chasing the wrong forest female into greenery from which I will not emerge unscathed. Maybe *sylph* or *dryad* but overlettered, likely too obscure *D&D* for this. *Fox*, instead? Or the vixen version, tracks of male and female crisscrossing exes in snow.

Number 43 across, four letters for "excited," good news, they got "agog," but that was it.

A few bits missing: piece of map, torn out as perhaps a scrap of paper or to house gum past pulverized and geocached for another finder. Knowing that we're allowed to take the magazines home, I do, but the safety information card's the real prize. I stole dozens for my collection in years past, pleased with the iconography, the odd illustration decisions. I envisioned later planes going down, the crowd, once bored, scrapping for a card, a crutch, a written revelation to clutch into the blur of their final moments. Traveling alone, do you choose another's heart to hold? Does it matter whose? Is it the one who most looks like the one you love? The one you had eyes for on this flight, even if these flirtatious semaphors never crest because where is there to go?

Two barf bags, one unmarked, the other "For Motion Discomfort and Baby Diaper Disposal." For deposit, either way. No need to return. I fill mine with snacks. And put it back. A surprise for someone sore-backed, weary, weepy.

I write mash notes to the future on napkins on planes and in airports and leave them for another future lover. An anonymous space makes us bold. We can hold so few, and only briefly.

Read this first. Or read this last. Or start at A or the letter that begins your name. Draw a card. These once were cards, but now they're bound. Choose one that sparks a memory. Skim until you're entertained. Mark your progress as you go. Read the Dear Defacers twice at least. Read this only once. Or read this not at all. Or start at the beginning but don't stop when you reach the end. Lay them on a table and read them all at once. Which one you choose augurs your future, reader, lover of the future. We have technologies to track where your eyes go.

Read the filthy ones, the ones with songs, the longest first, and then the short-est. You may, with a clean conscience, as Cortázar instructs in his *Hopscotch,* read some and discard the rest. Or, as in *The Unfortunates,* read the first and read the last, but the others can come in any order. Dip a toe and quit, or go full on cliff dive and summer skinny-dip. Do it until you're full or filled with ideas for what to write. Write in this book. Use this page. Here is a blank to fill:

. Play this like a game. Reading is participation, but I want more of you. So mark it up. Annotate a page. Trade a boring essay with another copy. Skim until you are compelled. Think of something else, like Beaudelaire, Apollinaire, *Jane Eyre,* someone with fair hair or a fine derriere. Read left to right, top to bottom, or its reverse. Be perverse. Read as the Greeks who plowed the field: out and back, *boustrophedon*. The way we read these days is just convention.

If you prefer direction, alphabetical's always good. Be good. Leave this as you found it. Or vandalize. Be bad. Steal a page. Take the whole home and roast it like a ham. Slide one in a book you lend or that you return. Better, make your own and publish it in a book. Make a box. Fill it with what you love or think or think you love. Install a card in the library at the Museum of Jurassic Technology in Los Angeles or Iceland's Library of Water, or whatever library you choose to use.

Then I shall explain them and illustrate them. (The rule, which we discussed in the last chapter, was: *Cla the book according to kind and subject matter*.)

The second rule—I say "second" because I want to the numbering of the four rules which comprise the way of reading—can be expressed as follows: *State the u of the whole book in a single sentence, or at most in se* sentences (a short paragraph).*

This means that you must be able to say what the w book is about as briefly as possible. To say what whole book is about is not the same as saying what kin book it is. The word "about" may be misleading here. In sense, a book is *about* a certain type of subject matter, w it treats in a certain way. If you know this, you know *kind* of book it is. But there is another and perhaps n colloquial sense of "about." We ask a person what h about, what he is up to. So we can wonder what an auth trying to do. To find out what a book is *about* in this s is to discover its *theme* or main *point*.

Everyone, I think, will admit that a book is a wor art. Furthermore, they will agree that in proportion as

—Mortimer Jerome Adler, *How to Read a Book* (PN83.A43 1940, University of Arizona Library, Main)

Oh, snap. All books may not be art, but they are books. The look of them. The feel of them: just paper in the hands & your hands moving through its odd habitual itinerary. Some readers check off chapters, tick off each paragraph as read, done, and over, over and over, just to be sure, hence the check marks in the margins of this copy. What am I sure of? Doves diving by the library window in search of something unknowable, then looping back again. The afternoon light through a wintry drear? The sudden attempt at focus of the students studying for finals, December, late afternoon, a Wednesday, every carrel suddenly, improbably in use? The cellular trill that interrupts the gaze? Reminders that conversations—

flattened into data—are in the air around us even if we cannot receive them? The ways we try to pay attention to what we know we ought but rarely can?

Our attempts at love come back to mind every other moment: how have we failed, and when did we know, and why does it come back to the brain like this? "To say what the whole book is about is not the same as saying what kind of book it is. The word 'about' may be misleading here," says Adler. But about is everything, a cup for collecting, a magnet gathering data from everywhere we can imagine into essay.

Every afternoon has a terror in it, opportunities for error, the hum of fair air through the ventilating shafts that terminate in slatted squares and spread our breath flat out across the floor. Everyone is breathing us. We are mouth to mouth, a study in resuscitation, the collective dioxide heft left over from our brains' effort. Then someone farts. A giggle.

The margin note is a spark of snark, the reader irritated enough to inscribe the space, not just with check marks and asterisks, glyphs of the age of type, the type of age we're in where a student asks me what font was the Declaration of Independence written in? And I say Comic Sans, sans wink or hint of anything but the epic fount of knowledge that I periodically tap on command and pour out, pearls overflowing in the hand. It was cheap, an easy out. I don't feel good about it.

Dear undergraduate, let me tell you about rage: the defacing of the pages in the university library makes me want to get my box cutter and rain terrorism on your wee, thonged heart. I am all for marginalia, and Adler argues for this, but save it for a book you own or wrote or at least hope to fill with interesting argument, your breath now alive with mint. Yes, I see you with the Altoid tins, the sugar stink, the price we pay for trying to think so hard for so long that everything is like *like*, pairable, easily associated, in comparison with another, slotted in a tube of convergence until it comes together or fails into obsolescence or meaninglessness. "Together" is a useful illusion, the artifice of the vanishing point. Nothing really ever comes together. Not us and those we love, I fear. We are on separate rails, magnetically opposed.

Some days I feel closed to the new, curled up in myself like an @, in Italian it's called *chiocciola*, curled snail. Where are we @ exactly? I mean it in the contemporary way, like are we here, shelved, libraried, haunted by thoughts of X and how she looked alone in libraries, caught in the trap of fantasy, or are we somewhere else instead, overhearing a breakup conversation, voicemail breaking up a carrel away, a generation away, a life away in dream already, on the verge of vanishing or already gone?

> My wife and son and I are about to leave. For an instant I
> glance at all the other people here and try to fix them into a
> scene of stationary, luminous repose, as if under glass, in
> which they would be given an instant of formal visual preci-
> sion, without reference to who they are as people. Even now,
> with the light changing, the sun moving more rapidly toward
> the horizon and the light gradually acquiring that slightly un-
> natural peach tint it has before twilight when the shadows are
> grotesquely elongated, I cannot do it. These people keep mov-
> ing out and away from the neat visual pattern I am hoping for.
> I breathe out, stand up, and walk with my wife and son to
> the car.

—Charles Baxter, "A Late Sunday Afternoon by the Huron," *Through the Safety Net*
(PS3552.A8543 T4 1986, University of Arizona Library, Main)

It's impossible, isn't it? To hold it all, strands in hand as if everything were fiber optic cable, gathered threads of glass: just one writer's ambition; a lifetime's in-formation sieved; another aching heart; an angry margin scrawler; the under-graduate napping between stacks escaping the squalor of his dorm; someone curious about what another's life might be like; a collection of come hithers mas-querading as short stories; stacked, hollow dolls of memory or memoir; *memoir* as scientific term (meaning *note, memorandum,* or *a record*); the ghosts of those who conduct paranormal research; old words, dead hearts perused occasionally at best by the body of a living reader, maybe you. Baxter knows: to even try to grasp a vastness such as this is foolishness.

We contain every search or text or bit of Internet Relay Chat carried over every lovely pulse of Wi-Fi or 3G in this space even if we're not aware of it: they occupy our brains for a microsecond electromagnetically before propagating on through flesh, mortar, and air to a recipient. I could be in any library (however tiny): they're all built upon the one before or the idea of the one before, like an in-visible, impossible, ineffable hotel, story upon story, unaware of the one below, possessing us.

There's no way to fix it, describe it, or even demonstrate its depth. At best I can only hold a hundred fragments touched by human mind or hand or heart and see what they suggest, and just for a moment—then they are swamped by some-thing new, a sentence here, Charles Baxter's youthful face, my fading vision, re-ceding horizon. I could use some rest. Is no one else impressed? Few readers here take note of such muchness except to sigh or burp or gasp in surprise or sudden pleasure—the subroutines of the body—or dog-ear or tear a page, too lazy to Instagram it or reproduce it in their commonplace. As the place shuts down at night and the librarians, daily operators and curators of all this information, stream home, they must know it's all an expanding folly. *But a necessary one,* they might say. Or *it's just a job, a place to work, some books, a place to go.*

Where do the defacers go, the salivating readers, the offended searchers, dead-end explorers, missed connections, the writers trying all day to make it new or not at all? Freed or forced to leave, we all stream home (some to our geodesic domes, this being only forty miles from the research facility at the Biosphere 2). We have our bodies after all, and they belong somewhere, with someone else, if we're lucky. And if our minds find another's in passing, a stranger's a decade or a century along, well, maybe that's enough: a way to leave a trace of us, who we were or wanted to be, what we read and could imagine, what we did and what we left for you.

I would gladly be a creative person if I could, but I fear it is my lot in life merely to organize and arrange what others have created. . . . It was only natural that I should begin to acquire books on [the gay liberation] movement. After I filled two shelves with books, all of which were marked HQ 76, with a Cutter number for the author, I began to realize that the Library of Congress had failed to make adequate provision for this subject. I decided I would make some changes.

—David Allen White, "Homosexuality and Gay Liberation:
An Expansion of the Library of Congress Classification Schedule,"
Hennepin County Library Cataloging Bulletin, no. 28, 35–38, 1977

Sometimes the forms we cleave to need revision. As in the television's thirty-minute blocks, the length of our commute, the familiar thought of His and Hers, driving on the right, our days are more structured by convention than we like to think. Dear David Allen White, I was married here, in Hennepin County, Minnesota, at the county courthouse, our wedding vows witnessed by a judge between cases of Criminal Sexual Conduct, Classes C and D.

Our errors are classified this way as felony or misdemeanor, minor, major, venal, incidental, mortal, thoughtful, supersexy, supermax. The cataloger knows you can't have coding without syntax, meaning without sorting, so how a book is sorted means and resonates beyond the shelves.

There's my wedding photo on the shelf. I'm all Alabama bulge and drinking neck, full from weekly trips to the Krispy Kreme just down the street where dough was hot and now and I was always hot to eat it now and so I did. But Megan stars in that bright dress: such loveliness! In what ways did I deserve this state-sanctioned shot at happiness, and what have I done with it? In Alabama we voted just a year before to legalize interracial marriage. It passed sixty to forty. Hard to take part in a thing still denied to friends, but knowing this we chose to stitch ourselves to each other and hold fast, make that joining mean.

That's how it starts: with a little thing, a decision made, a hack. A reclassification in a system spreads. Just a kludge, a snip of DNA to reduce the likelihood of your future sickness, an asteroid laser nudge to save a continent: what happens to the redirected? An accidental introduction shifts the ecosystem: kudzu to the south, Asian carp to the Great Lakes, buffelgrass to Arizona, Banana Bunchy top virus to Hawai'i, Europeans to the new world, Hi-Yo Silver on WXYZ radio in Detroit.

These words are just small, on cards, parasites riding inside the spines of books. But everything's a vector, even if I can't understand how or why it moves, how slowly, or where it's going to. Like bottled letters chucked into the water, I hope—or maybe trust—for a good current to carry this news as far as it will go.

Sometimes it takes a collector to make a difference in the system, adjust a filing algorithm, point out an oversight or error, suggest a shift. Don't worry, David Allen White: your reclassification is no less a creative act than that of novelists. It takes some provocation to prompt a beast that big to shift, to get the Library of Congress subject headings moved from "Sexual Perversion" into "Sexual Deviation," and to liberate "Homosexuality" from that container into the wider world of "Sexual Life." Never mind that these are incremental steps: what life is not sexual? we might wonder. Everything is form, but under stress a form will change, and should, because form's just history. The river overfills with monsoon rain and reroutes, collapsing a bridge ten miles out, and redirects itself.

Elsewhere in this cataloging bulletin there's a proposal to add a new subject heading for "Unnecessary Surgery," perhaps judging those who choose to have their sex reassigned to the one they always knew it was? From my arm I had a cyst removed the year before we left Tuscaloosa: the scar is still visible, the interloper gone. Almost a decade later tornadoes cut a one-mile swath through the Druid City and obliterated both our last house and the apartment we lived in, miles away, the year before. Photographs show there is nothing left of us and where we were, who we used to be, no evidence of our neighbor's house, like ours, built post–WWII for those coming back to school on the GI Bill. Alabama and eventual NFL quarterback Joe Namath once lived there, we were told by a pilgrim snapping photographs. Now that too is gone. The Krispy Kreme's rebuilt, but there's no remainder of the feral cats we fed and buried there, the friendships that we started, or those that ended.

Except for us, our pitch-shifting bits of memory and how we unreliably encode it, and what's here on this page or others, there's no reminder there or anywhere of our attempts, however small, to change or reclassify our world.

Yet twelve years later I can feel the vector moving. My friends Jon and Clint now have several states from which to choose to host their wedding vows: maybe even Arizona by the time this is printed. Twelve years later I still want a doughnut badly.

RAILWAY ACCOUNTING OFFICERS ASSOCIATION
Meeting at Atlanta, Ga., May 1-4, 1928

Fill in this slip and hand it to the Secretary

Name..

Title...

Road..

Everyone attending this meeting should register on this slip and hand it to the Secretary, prior to or at the time of assembling.
This is necessary in recording your attendance.

This Agenda is not intended to be authoritative or official. It is compiled by the Secretary merely with a view to facilitating the orderly conduct of the meeting, and to prevent matters, of which he has knowledge, from being overlooked.

—*Railway Accounting Officers Association Agenda for Fortieth Annual Meeting,* May 1–4, 1928 (HE 2241.A76 40th 1928)

I draw your attention to the five men memorialized at the end of the 289-page annual agenda, after the constitutional amendment and the bylaw changes, before the member roll call (stop me if this turns you on unduly—I know it's sexy) of the yearly meeting of the Railway Accounting Officers Association, punctual as punched dots in a piano roll. (Those piano—pianola—rolls were manufactured until the first Thursday of 2009, when QRS Music Technologies of Buffalo stopped the assembly line grind for the last time and everything was silent for a moment, then stayed that way.)

I marvel at the minor movements of the RAOA meeting, the thousand resolutions attending to such important matters as the variable acceptability of scrip books for the passage of circus performers or the properly esoteric process for reimbursement of half-rate sleeping card accommodations for "members of the Association and dependent members of their families who are not prohibited by law from accepting such reduced rates for the purpose of attending the annual meeting."

Such officiousness! At this, the association might quibble, dribbling coffee at my implication, make a motion to suggest *efficaciousness* instead to be more precise with meaning—these details are important, you understand: shift a decimal point from its location and a company is ruined, its tracks busted, rusting in the course of progress, its cars scrapped in heaps by the poisoned lake where the kids play, the brave ones, the ruined ones, the ones who don't know better or do but don't care. I mean to say the world is in the quibble, the instant, speck on glass, the movement of a mote in air, defunct but once iconic bit of slang. *Officious* now reads pejorative when once it stood, Ionic, glorious, for order—power and majesty of progress, the columned, tabulated world. Knowing this retains an order, holds a finger in the dike against the rising river, against erosion, the history of language, the history of human hands on books, those due dates in books' backs in the few libraries that still maintain the practice. Or perhaps by my saying this, I'm just being officious.

The inclusion of the memorial list of names is most important; because it dignified the life, it dignified the work: Carroll Preston Cooper ("a man of exceptional business ability"), John Arthur Robinson ("an able accountant"), William Aloysius Rooks ("an enthusiastic and active worker . . . one of the country's most capable and foremost freight auditors"), Isaac Gouverneur Ogden ("originated . . . the accounting system of the Canadian Pacific Railway . . . put it into practice, and finally perfected it"), and John Clark Thurman (who sadly merits no such praise).

Keepers of the sums and rules of order, you all died in 1928 but are noted in the record, on the record, and for the record, so long as it lasts, so long may it last.

OHIO UNIVERSITY LIBRARY: Please return this book as soon as you have finished with it. In order to avoid a fine it must be returned by the latest date stamped below:

QUARTE [   ]AN; Jan 3, 1991; Jan 6, 1991; Sep 7, 1994; QUARTER LOAN; Jul 18 1994; FACULTY LOAN; Dec 15, 1995; Jan 04, 1996; RETURN BY; Oct 08 1998; RETURNED Sep 06 2002; Sep 26, 1990; Oct 02, 1998; Sep 12, 2000; Apr 05, 2001; Jun 07 2000; Mar 07, 2001; Sep [   ] 2002; Sep 12, 2002; Jun 12, 2006

—Mahendra Kumar Jain, *Introduction to Biological Membranes,* 2nd edition (QH601.J36 1988, Ohio University Library)

Each space between the dates, a vastness, wind rustling palms through the space between them. Or should I note the oak instead just beyond the window screen from the seventh-floor Ohio window? Those palms are a year away by foot, less so by car or train or aeroplane, the US Postal Service's brief experiments with rocket mail, ski mail, or camel mail, just to name a few. I love books with date stamps for this history: the moments between one span of attention and another, sometimes years removed, marked indelibly in ink. The ritual of that stamp is now gone, replaced by scan, bar code; the old gives way to new, then, too, it's old, and we are old, and we fear no one will know to read the dates on the stones we choose to adorn our tombs. There are thousands here a few miles away at the former mental institution in Athens, Ohio, a library of stones, numbers but no names, their institutionalized, lobotomized brains secreted away, then erased.

Decay will take it all in time. It's not as if the brain remains the same as it was just yesterday. A chemical shift: a misremembered date, lost childhood artifact. *Factum:* thing done, past participle of *facere,* to do. So too with books, their pages now containing what? a dedication to the author's mother, "who once wondered why the evening news always lasts thirty minutes"? The deep science of this book paired with the human act of stretching toward another one. A good question too, why the thirty-minute chunk? What network force has formed our hours in front of televisions as long as most of us have been alive?

In the library, this flimsy wood carrel does not keep the world away. A pair of undergraduates whisper more loudly than they should *only an hour now until the zombie walk.* A cough could bring diaspora of virus from the next row over. What membrane separates this thinking from the thinking of the girl the next cell over, a book on hearing aids spread out like a lawn before her? From their body language, the whispering pair is only doubtfully a couple. The girl leaves. The last book she touched is *Hearing Aids*, by Harvey Dillon.

This interaction is exactly what I'm seeking: knowing someone was just reading this, that this book has history. That it falls open to a chapter on signal-to-noise ratio suggests the binding's broken in this exact way, that this page is the one the body slept on after its too long late-night engagement, or that the diagram on using "compression to decrease noise" gave someone pause to think or scan or photograph. Compress a thing enough and you squeeze the noise out of it, reduce it to its essence until it is irreducible beyond that point. The human voice, for instance. The human brain, for instance. If reduced enough they become just another pulp. All we do is process noise, the air-conditioned hum, the brush of wet boot on berber, the flirtations in the RC 552 (P67)-685 (H81-H767) aisle, leaves spiraling down in a slight wind, a breath, a hush, a shush, and soon the library and all its membranes (are we it? is it us?) will be ours for hours again.

This winter is in for a lot.

—Inger Christensen, "Winter," *Light, Grass, and Letter in April*
(University of Arizona Poetry Center Library, no. 39800)

Odd and sad that on page twenty-three of Inger Christensen it is necessary to occupy the white space with a stamp: "Property of University of Arizona Poetry Center." This and the morning light suggest that this book is in danger of being stolen. This morning is in danger too—of being filed away, unmarked, unlisted, uncelebrated, unfilled with words. How many mornings do I have left? On my left, outside, the "Steve Orlen Fountain," flat and wide memorial to the dead poet, spits its liquid epitaph onto rocks, unceasingly.

I left my laptop power brick plugged into this same outlet in the UA Poetry Center two days ago and found it here this morning, undisturbed, still humming slightly, warm, in a sun surround. Yesterday was cool for Tucson, July 4, monsoon rain and firework spark and boom above us, raining down trails of light all night. Christensen reminds me that "This winter is in for a lot"—from her poem

"Winter," in her first book, translated into English, published here a year after her death. You can see her starting the ascent to her masterpiece, *Alphabet*, in which she approaches eternity by iteration of all that which exists, in Fibonacci sequence.

The fountain says little in response: a water wash. If it could somehow smoke, it would be fitting. Orlen has been gone twenty months. I work in his former office, which stank of thirty years of smoke, even after cleaning and coats of paint. We were instructed not to smoke inside the building, but no one believed he cared. After he died, I salvaged a stack of his discarded manuscripts from seven boxes left out for the trash. It seemed wrong to let those words go without mention. In my small way I loved that man. Others did as well. His heart, it got around.

The water spills itself outside in shade. Eight bamboo, eight feet away, gain from its precipitation. My project here is iteration, too, to collect—also in my small way—a series of moments, objects, abject items defaced by human hands or processed by unspeakable machines a generation away from ours, and by so interceding in the march of hours, the process by which the world becomes obsolete and begins to fade, to make an echo, record, an impermanent reminder of what is and was and will be still here for another generation, yours perhaps, if we could be so lucky.

These things exist. Orlen existed and still does in trace, in memory of water. Christensen exists on these shelves, marked with these stamps. As a rule I don't recommend stealing from libraries, but you could do worse than to lift a book of Christensen's or Orlen's from these shelves and furnish your life with it. So I do.

To be marginal in Michigan, barely on the chart, our peninsula cut in half on maps to save space.

To be contained within four walls and to know a storm's beyond them. To see what happened to the world while I was reading and trying to keep the fire alive.

To walk along a periphery. To skirt a lake. To perambulate, to circumnavigate a shore, and all you know is shore. To want more. To know there must be something past the water boundary. Others might know it differently, understand this place from their perch adrift: a port, respite, a place to land.

To tread on emptiness. To leave a mark. To know it will be erased by snow.

To acknowledge that where I'm from is underwritten and underread, to know that such a place might as well not exist for anyone besides myself and those few who know of what I speak.

Not to be able to forget or ever leave, not really. To be permanently fogged by it, foxed by it like in a description of a used book, condition *good, minimal high-lighting, former library book, seen better days, free to good home.* To wonder what a good home is.

To inhabit ruin. To be known for it, our home a more dramatic relative of Detroit's spectacular decline. To know the place once was much more than this. To know that Calumet, peak population nearly 100,000, current population 712, was nearly made the capital of Michigan a century ago. It lost out to Lansing by one vote. At the time it was one of the richest towns in America, producing 82 percent of worldwide copper. Now the mines are (mostly) closed, the money (mostly) gone. Now it's (mostly) past we're living in, a ghost, a sense of ruination, of what was once and no longer is.

To know *mostly.* To feel we're on the brink of disappearing—or, on better days, becoming. To know our ruins remain a tour for tourists, a getaway, a winter playground for those who come. Our closed mines and hoists demonstrate time to you.

To know that we're alone out here, up here, in here. To hold dear that sense of loneliness. To hear that all the things happening are happening to others, in other, more populated places, warmer places, places with less winter, places with a future. I recognize it is an adolescent thought. Perhaps it is because I no longer live in Michigan that my relationship with it is frozen there.

But still the mine goes deep. The doors are closed but the passages remain.

To venerate the remainder, a reminder. To want to fill it but not know how.

To articulate a low-down song of longing.

To manifest resistance to those who'd choose to ruin our ruins, to those who choose to flatten us with their attention or their inattention. They're ours, these haunting hours, these wrecks, these dredges, these stamp-sand mounds, these closed and crumbling mouths.

To drink of and in the past.

To know that many of us who once did anything to leave end up coming back.

To not return, not yet.

To dream of it.

To keep singing.

self. We shall find that the observed cases fall broadly into four categories:—
1. First come messages neither definitely sensory nor definitely motor, but consisting of vague or anomalous impressions or impulses. 2. Secondly, we have messages mainly sensory, or passive automatism. 3. Thirdly, we have messages mainly motor, or active automatism. 4. Lastly, we have messages at once motor and sensory, which tend to occupy the whole psychical field, and to pass on into states of trance, or of alternating personality.

It is enough to show that a man's belief that his acts have been willed by his ordinary conscious self is no proof whatever that they have primarily been so willed. They may have been primarily willed by some subjacent stratum of his being—as in the case of the post-hypnotic suggestion—and may yet appear to his supraliminal self as absolutely of its own choosing.

This fact is that not only may these gaps in our superficial memory possess a chain of memory of their own, but that such secondary chain of memory is actually in some sense more continuous than the primary.

—Highlighted text from Frederic W. H. Myers, *The Subliminal Consciousness* (BF 1031 M885, University of Arizona Library, Main)

It must cease somewhere, that self, with a period perhaps, a red balloon aloft—a real red balloon, symbol for nothing more than a red balloon—and rising against the mountain. Look at it hang there, a moon, a marker, marvelous in its randomness. At what point might we attenuate, cut ourselves down to this, a few quotes highlighted in a library book? What might that have to say about the questions we had that day? Did we look for doubleness, an explanation for how we seem swayed against our own best interests, how and why we are not in control? Are our desires ours or are we theirs or suspended in between? What happened to the hours we spent in reverie, slaves to them? Could this passage be a message from the dreamworld we hope we dream we must know is just below or past this one? What is a self but a receiver?

Like Cocteau's Orpheus we tune our radios low and wait for communication. When it was new the radio must have seemed such magic: from apparent nothingness, a voice, a song, deliverance. It seemed that way to me in cars at night driving through snowstorms, heading home, hoping to pick something up to give the transitory hour some meaning.

Through its lighted dials I can understand how some believe in spirits, ghosts, faeries, God, or something else: if we can communicate through air, who's to say there's nothing else? I guess these highlighted passages are themselves a passage into past, darkness, another's heart, if just for the hour. The reading life and the waking life meet this way, and the consciousness pleasingly recedes.

The many valences of the reading we're doing overlap with another, widening circles in a pond, future lover, highlighter of texts, how apertures seem to open right in front of us every couple of pages, then close right up again. In those bright-lit moments we can see through to some connection we have with the other other, if that's not the drugs talking, if that's not our desire talking. Maybe it's always the desire, the drugs, the desire for drugs talking: is it ever us? On the bus it's obvious which is us and which is else. Are we talking to ourselves? Did we say that bon mot out loud? Are we feeling awkward now?

A lot of wow, that highlighted passage, that "It is enough to show that a man's belief that his acts have been willed by his ordinary conscious self is no proof whatever that they have primarily been so willed." The book offers other forces, subliminal, mysterious, the push of gods or demons from whatever beyond you presently believe in, but it's more important here to note that we are not our own. Or: not always. Or: we are ours, but we do not know what we contain. If we could know it all, ourselves, our selves, then our life would be a coma, series of commas searching for an exclamation point, a program hardly worth running on our mainframes. Could we love the future/could we have the future, lover, if we could know our motivations fully? When we open a parenthesis (how very like a receiver it looks, tilting up to sky (do we ever stop at sentence's end (or do we somehow go on—

Colby College Library, Waterville, Maine: Sigillum Collegii Colbiani Lux
Mentis Scientia

—Bookplate in M. Faraday, "On Holding the Breath for a
Lengthened Period," *London and Edinburgh Philosophical Magazine
and Journal of Science,* third series, October 1833

When in Maine, I had my chance but spent almost no time inside your walls. I
didn't have the wherewithal (strange how that word dates back to 1535: doesn't
feel so old inside my mouth). Instead I chose the stars and a week of gray rain.
Dear Colby College Library, do you still use the bookplate I happened on in
Arizona that adorns the *London and Edinburgh Philosophical Magazine and Journal
of Science,* third series, October 1833?

Found, in the book it adorned, an article by one Michael Faraday, presumably the
Faraday who invented the electric motor, member of the Sandemanian church,
discoverer of diamagnetism, the phenomenon underwriting the 2010 publication of "Magnetic Levitation of Large Water Droplets and Mice," from which
the following: "The mouse initially appeared agitated, and moved around dis-
oriented, seemingly trying to hold on to something," though the mice eventually
acclimated to the situation. It is a common modern problem.

I cannot check this codex out, it being old and a periodical, deteriorating with each
periodic read, contained as it is now in a box littered with paper fragments from
your deckled edges. The bookplate gives the history, tells me it once was yours.
The document in a book one shelf down, a volume of *Philips Research Report,* reveals it was received on October 1, 1969, from Martinus Nijhoff at The Hague along
with volumes of *Entomologis Experimentalis et Applicata, Enzymologia, Geophysical
Prospecting,* and the *Journal of Chromatography.* What graphs or ties these periodicals together in this order I do not know. Documents have their limits.

Future lover, that it is here a country away suggests that you sold it off, donated
it, sent it out for pulping. Perhaps you digitized it, pinned your hope on the per-
manence of binary. Or someone pilfered it, intentionally, accidentally, it doesn't
matter: either way it's gone. Years after I left, I found two books from my college
library in my collection, unadorned with DUE DATE stamp or card. I returned
them with a note. I thought that librarians must live for notes like this, folded
humble mea culpas, signed or not, from years before, light from distant stars.

Faraday's paper begins: "Gentlemen, THERE are many facts which present themselves to observant men, and which, though seen by them to be curious or interesting, and new to the world, are not considered worthy of distinct publication. I have often felt this conclusion to be objectionable, and am convinced that it is better to [unreadable due to wear] such facts, and even known facts under new forms, provided it be done briefly, clearly, and with no more pretension than the phaenomena fairly deserve."

To return the book—to steal it back, to liberate, and send it—would be presumptuous. Still I feel the need to tell you that I found it here and know you owned it first, and that you do no longer. It is a slow sadness to have had a thing and lost it: a spouse, a house, a child, a draft, a line of work, a life. Sometimes we are aloft without intention, levitating mice.

You were my birthday present; you came to the door—no one else was home, you said "lets celebrate." We dropped acid and went to the friend with the nocturnal monkey-like animal and made love for hours. I fell totally, naively in love, so when you took me home in the morning I cried. I thought—but did not say—how could you walk away from perfect love. You kissed my eyes & said "we love, we'll meet soon." I wrote poetry & drew my love passionately to you no longer caring if the love was returned.

You wrote you were coming. Filled with the innocent love of an eighteen year old romantic who'd never been in love, I made a dress of gathered silk & braided tiny strands of my hair.

We went to Randolph Park and left our friends on the golf course to be alone. You laid me down and kissed me and when you entered me I felt a passion like an uncontrollable, unthinking itch to pull you further inside me—a desire that seemed so close & yet not quite fulfilled. It was as if my entire self had been waiting for you, just you, and you were almost me, almost there, almost perfect, then it was—and I was totally blissful & whole & at that moment you cried "You're coming already." I was delighted

Turtle Island

My love, my lover,

Jon, LW, I'm dancing Wind
One lover's name, another lover's name.
From Marguerite Duras' novel
The Lover — the last lines:

"And then he told her, Told her that it was as before, that he still loved her, he could never stop loving her, that he'd love her until death."

Love, Paula

—Inscribed in Gary Snyder, *Turtle Island* (Casa de los Niños discard library)

Handwritten, it goes without saying, this inscription to an unnamed lover goes on for three pages before arriving at a final sorrow at the lover's loss—"today we are with different lovers"—but no regrets. Was it ever sent? Ever read? One thing is sure: it was inscribed and meant. Such passion cannot be shrugged off until it can. I found the book in Casa de los Niños on Prince and Mountain, thrift shop stuffed with this stuff, the stuffing escaping the chewed-on animals packed in the discount bin. Take six for a buck. Doll heads are free. They stare at your future, our future, maybe, lover, if we ever come together.

Dear future lover, every time it feels like forever when it's new: bright colors, fabric softener, calliopes that were once terrifying softening into daylight as it fades. You know, your lovers surely number more than mine; that's fine, but when I fall, it's Ditch Witch hitting electric line, the whole world alive and lit in amperes for a moment. It might be gone again a nanosecond later, the body aching with or for or from the jolt; & perhaps it's fever dream; & who cares where it comes from as long as it's fast and seems like it might last until we're rusting into dust? We are always dying for the future. Otherwise it couldn't ever come. That it might split ever's seams apart, that it might bring down the lights until forever's in the mirror, and the book is given up for thrift: it doesn't matter. Maybe this book was never sent. I can imagine that, an inscription toward the future. Maybe the lover's dead. Maybe the lover's lover's dead. Maybe we all are like those who had their laughs recorded into tracks for television shows years before, who continue to laugh now a lifetime a lifeline a phone-a-friend later, disembodied, at jokes that are no longer funny. Perhaps they never were.

We are all in wires eventually, reduced to what we said, or didn't say, and what we wrote or didn't write, who we loved or didn't love, or loved and lost and never told it except writing in or to a book. We are all discarded, discordant, confusingly, and so I salute your bravery, book inscriber. Your heart is big enough for both of us, so that there is no room for mockery in me. Anyone willing to strip themselves this bare this fast this way deserves our breathlessness and our hearts' attention. Let us spend an hour, then longer, in contemplation. If you open, open all the way, or as much as you can bear, or else there's nothing here at all.

The inscription goes on to quote from Duras's *The Lover,* then "I cried when I was with you this time more than twenty years later. . . . It was the reason for life and yet I knew it would end."

A codex is a door, future lover. You can put whatever through it for a reader you imagine coming to your words in a day, a decade, a daze of centuries, entries in a future book. Codices have histories. They are leafed, spined, embodied, read by future lovers I imagine in bodices in just this kind of light at night. The future is a mystery, lover, a memory. The scent of wisteria coming up from somewhere.

Or: a codex is a hole through which we might not communicate, but instead be transformed entirely, through which we might descend without notice or equipment and not want or be able to return.

Time -- on the order of several years -- is necessary to plan for this sort of change. If the decision of the Library of Congress on this matter remains in doubt for the indefinite future, it is likely that several other major libraries will decide on a catalog cutoff within the next year or two. As a result, increased diversity in cataloging practices and policies, and increased difficulties in merging of records for a national bibliographic data store may well occur. In view of the multiple advantages to research libraries and their users which might accrue from closing catalogs in concert with the Library of Congress, a thorough examination of the questions, and a consequent decision (or series of decisions) should be attempted at the earliest possible date.

—The Future of Card Catalogs (Z693.A15 F88)

You too must love the past if you are here. In the days of the digital, our fingers both touched this page. Oils on skin commingle here, in this spread, my head, this empty stage. See how a page contains a stain from something on a facing page? We too echo and leach into one another. My fingers were here, verso, and yours, recto as we turned this leaf together, and in another world our hands might have brushed. Instead there is this, missive to you, miss or mister reading in a mist, future reader, lover of all things past, all things codex, ex libris, body, spine, spirit, artifact. Let's get physical for a minute (yes, that is a reference—all my language is a code for a certain sort of reader): dead skin, trace finger oil, the coworking of our eyes (all eyes leave a trace: how can they not?) along this particular line of type. Residue from the breath, perhaps a hair or a fingernail, a spot of blood, of sweat, of tear—all this is body is what I'm saying. Who knows what other bit of me might have been here? I am a body. I was a body until I was not. I was a body who cradled this book in my hands, held it for a moment, meant only for one other at a time, like a sentence, like a kiss. I mean to say this is for you, dear ex, dear past, dear reader with a body, reader with a brain, here unnamed. I might have limned it in a dream. I promise not to say *limn* again. It's too filled with poesy, stuffed doughnut of pomposity—though do not spell it *donut*. That betrays the history of language. I admit that I am not so full of love for the history of language. Much of it, like dead skin, is disposable: *who* and *whom,* for instance. Holdovers from the Latin like split infinitives, for instance (though I understand it is now acceptable to split infinitives in mixed company, provided you are drunk and have removed at least one item of clothing). Maybe by the time you read this you'll not know the distinction either. Maybe it will, like the prevalence of reading in the young, we're told, soon be gone.

I cannot know the world you inhabit, past lover. What I know is that there was once this thing we called the future, and we were wrong about it mostly, surely; slowly it became obvious in what ways we had mispredicted, worried at the wrong issues, loved on the wrong aspects of artifact, misunderestimated the flexibility of future language and its strategeries, its nucular power when wielded premature like a banner on an aircraft carrier, or like a welding torch of a polemic, blasting vision from your retinas for weeks. We might have been too caught up in hypertext, the future we envisioned for text and book and story thirty years before or more, and still continued fiddling with, mostly without payoff or linguistic, autoerotic pop, while everything else rusted.

What is the future like, past lover? You're here, so you too must trust the past: all those fights, all those pages. Some not all that old, some older. These libraries were once meant for something. They held the knowledge of the age. What is it to be a body, a body with a spine, holding another body in our hands? What is it to love a body? To love a book? To love an artifact? To embed another in memory, analog or digital? Are we embodied? In what preferred gender pronouns are we contained? In which do we choose to contain ourselves? A friend asks to be referred to not as *he* but *they*. In this time—a personal time, I feel obliged to note, not wanting to speak for the entirety of the age—I found this odd. This suggests the rest of us were just plain ole I, with our stable spidey sense of self.

It's never been like that. Of course that I is multiple. I has always been a string of paper dolls, unfoldable to a multiple, uncountable choir, but ergonomically (I is just a convenient handle on a sack of otherness & unknowability) and maybe aspirationally we just say I, as if addressing a monolith. To privilege the multiple is to discount the multiplicity in all of us, I wanted to say, and did, because this human is my friend. Acknowledged, she said. *She* would be fine, or *sie* or *zhe*, whatever else, works: just not *he*. Okay, said I (said we?) to they, to she, I can get with that. *He* feels confining; I don't like it either. I've never felt fully comfortable with what it connotes, assholes with mancaves and a little biology and millennia of socialization and fuckuppery. I meander. I recognize it. I can see myself in the mirror waving, waving. Echo? Echo.

Are we contained in we? can we be penned into an I? manifested on pulped trees or magnetic fields like this? contained by the ways in which we express our Is? How we might believe our eyes, or might choose not to, preferring something beyond the rational: manifestation of the supernatural, meaning ghosts or God or maybe the irreducible mystery of language, the megalith underneath this sentence, every sentence, every hour. Yes, it's grandiose. But in the absence of my voice or quickened pulse I wanted you to know I thought of you.

—Cover of a rebound copy of Clifford D. Simak, *A Choice of Gods,* 1972
(Warwick Melrose Hotel Bar Library, Dallas, Texas)

There are few books here at the library in the Warwick Melrose in Dallas, Texas, and fewer meant for reading. Instead: a bar (and hardly the only one so named to accommodate excuses: *I was at the library all day, Dad, brother, professor, wife, lover, concerned observer*), and adorning it, only two small walls of books from which I grab a title. The pages are bound closed: instead I find a menu for the bar, the former bar (though it opened in 1924, this hotel's no longer Omni—has been the Warwick Melrose since 2007). So would anyone be concerned if I took this title home? Surely these haven't left the shelves in a decade, maybe longer. I grab another, *The Highlander,* yearbook for Highland High School, Albuquerque, New Mexico, 1955, half-filled with inscriptions to Bob Rice with little variation: ten deem him a "real nice guy"; five a "real swell guy"; only four a "real neat guy"; only two signed "love"; and clearly neither meant it. One goes so far as to tease the loveless Bob: "I love ya, I love ya, I love ya, Don't get excited, I love monkeys too," signed in an exceedingly and unreadably tiny female scrawl.

Excellent cursive and misspellings abound. There is no evidence here that anyone knew him well; perhaps that's why I find it on this shelf. Texas Bear Round Up 18: Casino Bear Royale is taking place a mile away this weekend, but no bears are in evidence at the library. Instead it's what you would expect: young bros discussing hegemonic topics, their latest sales, the status of their tuxes, trading *'sup*'s and jibes about their disappearing hair, how drunk they were, the travails of the NCAA. One gives another shit. A back is smacked. I know I'm being ungenerous but Miami Sound Machine is playing overloudly (which is to say at all) and no one is reading books or acknowledging their presence. From 1995, Nicholson Baker confides, in "Books as Furniture," that "books fill vacant spaces better than other collectibles because they represent a different order of plenitude," even when they're just used to list the single malts.

Two inscriptions from the *Highlander* deserve special mention for a modicum of wit: "To a good guy, from a better one" (signed Eddie Johnson) and "Don't do anything I wouldn't but if you do name it after me" (signed Zach Hockinson). Props to you, dudes from nearly sixty years ago, even if you honed your bons mots and awarded them in wasted spaces due to be discarded. I know you can't give everyone your full attention. Some of what we expect to be retrievable goes absentee instead: the categorization's fucked, the subject heading's gone, the indices or pointers misdirected, the book or the memory's misplaced if not erased. What we'd prefer to disappear resurfaces instead: lyrics to a pointless bit of Taylor Dayne, first name of our eighth-grade nemesis, the syntax of the idiot interactions we've had with friends (like those of bros, when seen en masse, I too am an easy target), the bro hug you gave the writer that he called you on, deeming you perhaps a bro (therein may lie your irritation with this festive group), the failure litanies we run through every night, desires, dissents, descents, desserts ordered and regretted.

It's best to consign all of this to trash, To Be Deleted, discard pile, the resale or remainder bin, except we live in a recorded and collected world. In that case bind them closed with glue, consign them to a hotel bar where they'll persist (they'll still exist: you're not yet willing to actively redact your past) but remain unread, until they don't. Or nuke it from orbit or chuck it into the volcano, thus saving Middle Earth in middle school. Is it redundant to add "without a trace," since that which leaves a trace is not entirely disappeared? Tell me, bros! Oh bros, you too will disappear in time. Your inscriptions to each other are already fading, like light from destroyed stars (I know it's a disaster). You too have names, I know, though I don't know them. You too have inner lives, if not yearbooks (those have mostly disappeared). You too were once "real swell," "real neat," "real nice," backwhacked, unloved, except in secret, tangential, ornamental to someone, maybe everyone. You too might have died or not been archived before I paid enough attention.

—Amaranth Borsuk and Brad Bouse, *Between Page and Screen*
www.betweenpageandscreen.com

Dear future lover, in this moment the future feels like this, somewhere between, as this book is titled, page and screen, the ways and means of making meaning. The codex itself has but little text. A die-cut cover. Just this pixel hex / these hieroglyphics. What is text but a set of glyphs, I know, but not all glyphs resolve so easily into language. Maybe you remember the pixelated bits from John Conway's "cellular automaton" *The Game of Life* (if not, you've probably got a screen, so perform a search), pixels representing "a collection of cells, which, based on a few mathematical rules, can live, die, or multiply." Hit start on the simulation and watch the pixels flower. Some configurations quickly go extinct. Others grow then fail into the white space of the margin. A few stabilize and repeat in an oscillating pattern, until the machine on which they're simulated ceases simulation.

To read this glyph above, this book above, we're directed to the website above. First, will we give the site access to our webcams? it asks us. That's kind of hot, we think, saying yes, and we wonder: what new intimacy is this? The site displays us now. Hold the glyph up to the screen; no, not that way; there; and on that screen, that image of our self, the machine projects a text: a poem, one of a set of correspondences between P and S, page and screen, perhaps, lovers, probably. As we manipulate the glyph on camera, the text moves with it, with us, our hands on a chimera. We hold it and we don't. We're holding something with no weight.

It's a rush, that intimacy, how it involves / evokes / actually pictures us. We read our bodies on the screen holding the book, appearing to hold the text, and in this way we read it. As one poem ends: "opn dor nto an otr room." The room onscreen is our room but not our room, our books, our stupid hair, our air for breathing, approximated via pixel, we know: some combo, an otr, an other room. This poem is written in the language of stock symbols, ticker-taping across our onscreen bodies. Its subscript and superscripts call the rise and fall of prices as in real time, suggesting the performance of those two stocks: page and screen. What's between them? we asked. Turns out that hinge is us.

Like mirror script, to read requires reflection, asks us to see ourselves holding the page. Wilde: "It is the spectator, and not life, that art really mirrors." Do we read books to see ourselves in others, in others' words? Or do we read to lose ourselves inside another? This book / site / otr space makes us work for this calculus, and it's hard not to see in this one future for the book: not obsolescence for one or the other, but a fused existence. Yeats tells us, epigraphed by M. H. Abrams, "It must go further still: that soul must become its own betrayer, its own deliverer, the one activity, the mirror turn lamp."

This book's trick bewitches mostly as proof of concept, what might be done to inform the way we read screen and page, not necessarily to set the one against the other. What if it asked the reader to perform some further inquiry into the self and its infinity of mirror games as we read text and self onscreen? What if it streamed video of others reading, how they contorted, what they wore, how they looked, if they looked like us, read like us, if there's any chance they might, like, go to the dance with us next week, please check the box either yes, maybe, or no?

The (networked) screen offers us the literalization of the social / share / the ease of collecting one avatar of self and superimposing it onto another. Already we network when we read. How stable must a text be to be a book? What if the digital text is not the same each time when we call it up? How stable is a sentence, anyhow, if when we return to it a decade later a novel calls us out anew? Anyway, what are books? Is this a book or just a cable box? Must it be bound to be a book? Are bound things bound to be a book? Must it (just) be print to be a book? Any text must earn its form if it wants my respect / my sex / my intellect. How is what it does best served by what it is? This play between this book / this screen / and us strikes me as a stable life-form, one worth repeating.

—Don Cowen, *Archimedes at the Battle of Syracuse, 212 BCE* (painting on loan from
Drs. Aden and Marjorie Meinel, University of Arizona Science & Engineering Library)

What is it about a mirror that works to hold our gaze? We're certain of ourselves
until reversed or made grotesque in hotel light, every blackhead on our blockhead
body highlighted, each crease accentuated. Science says we're built to see ourselves in everything, everything in ourselves (or is that just Narcissus speaking
through story, through science?). So you will search for yourself in this. You can't
not. We're excited by the human form. Our own, of course—a woman mastur-
bating in a mirror, searching out her own expression as she comes—but that of
others, too. Some of us are aroused by hiccups, so that any paroxysm starts us up.
Studies show the eyes of men are drawn (maybe unfortunately for men, to be so
simply driven) to the crotches of other men, chimpanzees, horses, dogs, even the
crux where two trees cross. It's crass and gross—so animal—to know that when
we see a human lying on the grass we'll gravitate to the crotch. Thanks, biology.
Civilization is a game of keep away with what we're drawn to do. Alive means
embracing inevitability, our baser natures, self-abasing, -abusing, -genuflecting,
-blogging, -help, -analysis.

This painting depicts "the first large-scale use of solar energy," two dozen centuries ago, to disorient the Romans: what a shock it must have been for them,
not just reflected, concentrated sun, the blind of sudden heat, but the bind of self,
approaching, swords up, propagated out, made multiple, by mirrors. That much

me would scare the hair off a bear. Hold up a mirror at the meeting to the bloviating dude, and see what happens. I just want you to see what you're saying, my wife says, and I rarely do. I kind of can't track that cant in that moment. Instead: deny. Think about it for a year. Let it percolate into a canto, canter, then speed up to gallop, word that feels like a palindrome but isn't, until it achieves full-on self-lacerating, ramming speed, and squeezes itself out in an essay.

I didn't mean to make this about myself, there's so much interesting history happening in the painting, and that it's on loan to the library from a private collection of the Meinels, for whom the Optics building across the street is named, so they're interested in light and how it can be made to work, most certainly. And is it strange to say I only noticed it when I put my head up against it, on the chair in front of it, and wondered: Should I be touching art? When did I last wash my hair? Is it (art, not hair) insured? Is it (art, not hair) any good? Do I like art? Do I like this piece of art? How many might have noticed it at all? At least I make my peace with it and run my hand along its frame.

Here in Tucson, the land of concentrated summer sun, it makes sense to think about the way we might harness infrared to do our bidding like a djinn (*jinn* and *jin* are also acceptable, for those in search of words beginning with a *j*). Its solar heart mirrors our solar hearts, the ways the undergraduates tan and squawk and strut, exchanging AmIHotOrNot.com passing glances and unsubtle flirts, the mutual checking out that suffuses days spent in libraries when we should properly be otherwise engaged in games of *Words with Friends* as we avoid our work, surrounded by evidence of intelligence. It's impossible to believe the dark will come on days like this, that all of this will end.

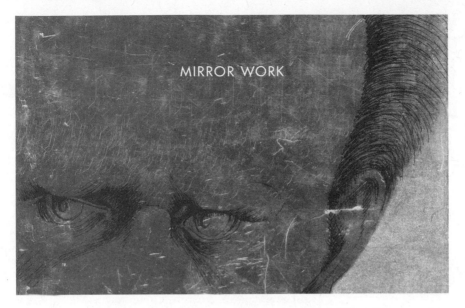

—Michael Ayrton, *Fabrications* (AC8.A95 1973, personal library)

In this book cover you might see yourself if positioned properly. Though you may experience it as gray, the silver here's a mirror. Facing Ayrton's cover (which he designed and illustrated), I see myself in his forehead expanse. Like a snowed-in field it conceals a hush. Like a long winter it contains a secret. Like the north it says nothing back when asked. Like skin, like analog, the scratches register the decades' passing, but though he died in 1975, this book, this simulation of the operation of his head's as fresh a labyrinth as any.

Author of *The Maze Maker,* and maker of the world's largest extant life-size concrete maze, commissioned by a reclusive millionaire, now deceased, in New York's Catskill mountains, when Ayrton saw himself I believe he saw himself as Daedalus. That is to say we see ourselves in myth, which is why it persists and resists attenuation.

My forehead also abounds. I don't fully see myself (except when I hold myself to a mirror—and even then do we really see ourselves or do we see reverse and wonder at our mirror other?) in him, in the bronze hymns he sang to the story of the labyrinth and the hybrid beast contained therein. His eyes allude to torment. Perhaps he wonders why his ear is torn. He cannot change the object of his gaze, even as it bleeds off the page. In this he speaks to me though nearly forty years have passed.

In 1989, in Republic, Michigan, and Clam Lake, Wisconsin, two small towns you probably wouldn't know except to travel through, Project ELF, an antenna apparatus for extremely low frequency radio communication, came online for the first time. It allowed the US Navy to send messages, via eighty-four miles of above-ground transmission line antenna, to submerged nuclear submarines over half the world, to preserve our first-strike capabilities, to preserve the possibility of response in case we were attacked. The data rate was slow; the messages were short; it transmitted only and could not receive; a three-letter code could be sent in fifteen minutes at 76 Hz. That is enough, if necessary, to obliterate a world.

How safe it is, is another question. Wisconsin fought its installation. Upper Michigan fought its installation. Texas fought its installation. All successfully. Until after twenty years of organized resistance a scaled-down ELF came online, orders of magnitude smaller, consisting not of buried lines but those that hung above the ground.

With it, in twelve hours you could transmit a tweet. A long story in a year. A lifetime wouldn't be enough to convey a brain through ground and air, weather and water. I mean to say it takes awhile to get a message through. I won't stop trying.

Late one night, after a prolonged discussion alleviated by whisky and water, I entered his workshop and found to my surprise that he had suspended my open book from an intricate structure of rods and clamps rising from turntables, which so disposed it that the text was revealed between two semi-translucent sheets of a shining neutral material which possessed the power to reflect the words. . . . By siting my book between two related sheets of this translucent yet reflective material, placed at carefully calculated angles to the text, he was able to elucidate the verbal matter and at the same time see his own image agreeably reflected and multiplied almost to infinity through the text.

—Michael Ayrton, *Fabrications* (AC8.A95 1973, personal library)

In this then you might see yourself if positioned properly. I mean by this a book, a cover, pages, a narrative, an afternoon, a life. Is that what we desire, the apparition of the I? In another book, Oliver Spurgeon English and Gerald H. J. Pearson's 1941 *Emotional Problems of Living*, I find "The child" replaced by a handwritten "I" in this sentence: "The child who has made a satisfactory adjustment in his infancy and childhood will nevertheless have some difficulties of adjustment in adolescence because the development of his ego is still far from complete and also because his superego may be still too much a simple reflection of the parents' attitude during childhood and not yet sufficiently modified by the influence of the social organization."

In this then you might see yourself if positioned properly. I have questions about echoes. Do you too?

In this then you might see yourself if positioned properly. Raise the page like a mirror to your face. An I flipped remains an I. Trace your lips along the page and practice this kiss. I was here before. Now leave your lip mark there.

In this then you might see yourself if positioned properly. Look at it from the past, for instance. You once placed notes in bottles and threw them in the lake and hoped. Once you found someone else's note. A phone number was attached, but it just rang and rang.

In this then you might see yourself if positioned properly. I see a fragment of myself in Ayrton, British artist, polymath, sculptor, noted maze-maker, devotee of

Daedalus, "the technician," novelist, and sometimes poet. From here he looks flatter than I'm sure he was. Maybe instead I see my father, fatter in a refracted mirror. As a child looking in my father's looking glass, in his beer glass that resonates as I ting it with a tine of fork on a summer evening, wondering about where echoes go, I hear the note come back off the cabin wall, hello to my hello. I watch myself with curiosity. There's so much that I don't know about who I was: can I say I even am that same myself of three decades ago?

In this then you might see yourself if positioned properly. Do you see yourself in I? Or do you lose yourself in I? Do you see me in yourself? (Are you hearing me in yourself? I am activating your inner ear with this sentence.) What are you here for, anyhow?

In this then you might see yourself if positioned properly. I don't mean this sexually. What are we made of if not of sex, towering glissandos of flesh rubbed at a certain angle and velocity?

In this then you might see yourself if positioned properly. Is siting my book—is ceding my book—is seeding my book—is reading my book—is leaving my book in other books a dissipation of its charge? A self distributed, reduced to its component parts? Is it breaking up its hard shelf ice? Will it suffice? Will anything rub consciousness away?

In this then you might see yourself if positioned properly. Breaking up, we're told, is hard to do. It's not as if I only wanted this, these bits: I wanted everything to be included. But try to get ahold of it.

In this then you might see yourself if positioned properly. In still summer August Upper Michigan air, in memories of explosions, in boyhood Franklin W. Dixon revelations, in Revelation 1:3: "Blessed is he that readeth . . . and keep those things which are written therein."

In this then you might see yourself if positioned properly. Think less of content, more container. These sentences are here for you alone.

In this then you might see yourself if positioned properly. If not of books, if not of boxes, if not of libraries or echoes, if not of lines of text paper-chained together, then of what are we composed?

This is my inclination as well, to pull it all into a spine, or spineless, as I recognize this is, disordered, as this also is, to include something of everything, or enough so as to suggest the capacity for holding anything. That this disconnected set of cards could collect a thousand pages and barely register a brush with the world, having taken the tiniest scraping from it, is humbling in every way.

Note the tear above on the upper left. The copy of the sheet was fastened inside this binding of the journal. Bind in everything, the instructions said, so the binder did. I tore it out, thought to carry out the spirit if not the letter of its instruction; no need to include the evidence of its own binding, process by which a trade magazine like this becomes a Library Book, suitable for preservation. Meta-, a shell, the trace of its construction seemed too much to bear in the text itself (*Hovering Craft and Hydrofoil*, issues from 1969 and 1970), so now it's gone, and only the tear remains.

The binder could have done much more: bound in the hearts of those crushed by what they thought was love (were they so wrong?) on these premises; bound in the memories of authors remaindered and discarded, sold by the Friends of the Library at their quarterly events; bound in the reading history of the writer whose work was anthologized and is no longer, shaved out of the *Norton Anthology*, who still frequents these uncomfortable reading couches. What of the readers who discovered Fluxus here, Calvino and Woolf here, Cortázar's *Hopscotch* here, and had their brain dismantled and then reassembled? Would that we could bind these strands in here too and hold them for a moment, for the future.

Dear reader, know this: that I did not liberate this sheet without deep thought. As I paused above the spread, I may have dozed for a moment, lost track of where

I was, who I was, when, and why, and I believe the spirit of this library found me then, in this moment out of time, and telegraphed its blessing to take the sheet. Normally I don't behave like this. Okay, sometimes I behave like this. It's not too much to note temptation.

You understand that this place breathes, expands, contracts with cold and breath, the infusion of new words: it yet shows signs of life in spite of what you've heard about the young and their reading habits. Treating a library as a crematorium for yesterday's knowledge does no one any good. Instead let's keep it live, a starter for your homemade sourdough, here for both of us, to take from it what we can and may and will, to allow it to grow inside of us, so that when we leave its premises it still embraces us, molds to us like lace or a virus heart, so that we might think the world a library and by so thinking, and our feeling, and our stealing, and our starting something new here, make it so.

I-ARC-3 RUSSIA A359. Issued in 1940 to commemorate the exploits of the officers and crew of the icebreaker *George Sedov,* which drifted in the Arctic Basin for 812 days. . . . The drift of the icebreaker on its scientific expedition is plainly shown on the map, which was charted from information recorded during the course of the observational voyage. The portraits of Captain Badigin and First Mate Trofimov and the crew, which make up the border of this regular postage stamp, impair somewhat the effectiveness of this map of the Arctic, nevertheless, it is still a Class I stamp map. The projection used in this instance was the stereographic.

—William R. Horney, "Miniature Maps of the World," *Weekly Philatelic Gossip* for August 14, 1948 (Call #: JOURNAL *Weekly Philatelic Gossip,* Peggy J. Schlusser Memorial Philatelic Library)

It's far too small to see detail from the tiny reproduction of the stamp in *Weekly Philatelic Gossip.* An inch across at most, what use might be made of a map like this? As Horney notes, "This depiction of the North Pacific Ocean is purely incidental to the four-motor plane above it. The map, produced by a series of heavy horizontal lines, is ill-defined, and for the most part, is inaccurate. Issued in 1947, this stamp is Korea's first air post." Air post's a good fit for stamp as map, since from above the world is more easily taken in, en route to a mailbox in Tucson, Arizona, in the year to come, illuminating the breath of globe.

What wonder was opened up by the foreign coins and currencies my father kept from his years abroad—spent in Côte d'Ivoire or Morocco, he and my mother wandering Africa in the 1970s, first in the Peace Corps then on their own. I'd dump the bag, spread them on the bed and marvel, wonder at their wander, this evidence of their exotic, former lives before they settled down in Upper Michigan and made another life. Then when my mother died at thirty-three, the borders of my father's life blurred, became inaccurate, her memory in part contained in coins like this. When young, I was aware that there were places away from the frozen heart of Upper Michigan through these foreign coins and books. Like many children I played through a series of hobbies, wondering which might stick and anchor me in the world: rock polishing, philately, numismatics, mathematics, the early days of telephony, Boy Scout merit badge collection, gymnastics, piano, soccer, vandalism. That list goes on. Childhood is collection, when the world feels open: there are so many blanks to be filled, explored, and sorted. Then at thirty-seven, confronted by a tiny map in an obscure journal, I realize I've never been most places, wonder why the thought doesn't make me want to travel.

Horney's list this week collects the seas, Group III, as collected on stamps. As of this date the Indian Ocean had not been printed on a stamp at all. Like the world, that would soon change. A previous map, I-W-1 Canada A33, "Issued to commemorate the introduction of penny postage throughout most of the British Empire, effective December 25, 1898, has been written about as much, if not more than any stamp ever issued. As a map of the British Empire it is now out of date, but appropriately, it is the first, and, if not the best, it was then the most complete map stamp of the whole world. Designed by the then Postmaster General of Canada, it was intended to acquaint Englishmen in the home islands with the vastness of the overseas dominions." May we remember then how maps—and stamps—foreign coins—families—genealogies—lives—are backed by systems, made in, of systems. Their marks contain our fathers' hearts. Never shall they part.

After spending 25 years in the memory business, I thought I had seen all the innovations that were possible in terms of how to make memories faster.

—"Memoir Systems Writes the Next Chapter on How to Increase System Performance," *BusinessWire*, October 3, 2011

First, it is too slow. In the age of speed, faster memories are better memories: "Memoir's technology can also lower embedded memory area and power consumption, and shorten memory development time." "Memoir" here is Memoir Systems, a company working on advances in memory encoding, decoding, and accessing technologies. It's an odd name for a memory company: though memoir and memory are troubled codependents, the sort of memory they're interested in is error-free, or nearly so, one or zero, glossy, electric, perfect, the sort of accuracy that would render memoirs as dull and pointless as dust, which in a house is mostly bits of human skin.

A home is a machine made for memory. I am on a plane above the flat white grid Midwest. Flash forward: when we land and visit my wife's family's home two hours from now for an early Thanksgiving, two photographs will be propped up on the buffet in the living room: one of my wife as a child, and one of her brother; they're both candid, sledding in snow, happy in the usual way, looking to the camera. They will have replaced the airbrushed high school senior shots. These memories are getting younger by the year.

A few feet away will be the coffee table—I remember when they got it, only a couple of years into our relationship, and like many memories, this wood is only indexed in terms of she and I, in the way that inevitably we locate songs associatively, who and where we were that year. It's "distressed," meaning scarred, imperfectly finished, so as to show its memory as tree, not as place to put your feet. This too is artifice, effect, a trend. I could go on, laminating every object with a thought, indexing them this way.

Fast-forward further and our selves split, paths fork. In one future the table might be left to us. In another it burns with all of us atop it, avoiding the approaching horde. In another it's mistaken for a tree and reinserted pointlessly into the ground. In another we're not here to run our hands along its grain because we've perished in a bridge collapse fifteen miles away, dying in the Mississippi. In another, no one's left; the world devolved to irradiated dust: it's all distressed. It's easy to imagine a thousand future ways in which our objects might be re-memorized. Memoir Systems seeks to minimize the number of forks and operations, and streamline the ways in which memory can be accessed by the processor calling things up through algorithmic encoding.

Approximately thirty-five thousand feet below me at the moment, though, I can see the angular meander of telephone poles with telephone lines and power lines, as it follows what must be an invisible road through Nebraska. A minute later all is obscured beneath a sudden layer of the most boring sort of cloud (the flat, gray sort, I don't know the name offhand: not cirrus, nor cumulus or cumulonimbus, tabloid sex bombs of clouds—that these things remain from lessons learned is itself a glory). This is memory. There and then it's not, not retained exactly and not unretained. You can't restrain it either when it comes. Sometimes you can see through it to what's beneath, what frames it, what screens it, scrims draped over limbs in the backyard just visible in the moonlight, an undressing woman behind. But detail eludes. Then detail comes, but wrong: the lining of your mother's heart-shaped jewelry box, one of only two things of hers you promised to retain after her passing, and losing the jewelry box or maybe giving it away, trying your best to give her up, to give that obsession up so she might not be made to haunt your prose. At least you have the other thing, which will go unnamed.

You were proud of using that image in a story—the heart-shaped box and all its easy metaphor—in the year you took your own senior photos, just before you heard the Nirvana song, and that was that; it was used and done to you. You can't even recall a lyric from the song right now, and you know it was cliché, your story, box the shape of a heart (not to mention inaccurate: hearts are lumpier), but it was still your mother's heart-shaped box, and perhaps it held her heart with you never knowing, like in a story, which she mostly is to you now, these decades later, either a story or a silence, or both, a story concealing a silence in its center, the sort shaped like a heart, the sort shaped like an unprompted, algorithmically encoded memory.

Skeleton of Megatherium.

—*The Harmsworth Encyclopaedia in Eight Volumes*, vol 6. Mark–Poetry, 1921
(Coffee Inn English Language Library, unsorted, Vilnius, Lithuania)

When wandering old encyclopedias, among the many wonders, wonder first at which entries bear a drawing and which do not. I get why *poetry* does not, but why diagram *cyclone* but not *monsoon,* or offer a portrait of Molière and not Monet, *mugwort* but not *mudar,* or instead of *Megalosaurus,* we get *Megatherium, skeleton of,* "an extinct fossil edendate of large size, allied to the existing sloths and ant-eaters . . . as large as an elephant"? A skeleton's a kind of diagram of an animal, a hopeful one, a doubtful one taken from a dream filtered through the available evidence, what we once thought this beast might look like if re-assembled, with its huge, prehensile claws resembling hands.

You can see the human in it. In assembling skeletons we often build ourselves again, our fears, what we imagined the world before us might be like. Of course it would be terrifying, filled with fear and threat for us. We should be happy to be living now, not born to run from thunder. Like it we too are tenuous.

Did you resemble this illustration, dear *Megatherium?* Were you more sloth, or closer to a bear, as research since this book suggests? Was your world filled with sadness or with hope, if you knew what those things were? Could you sense it passing like a northern summer or did you glory in it, stripping bark off trees, terrifying smaller beasts as a game to pass the time? If you knew you would be modeled by a company called Paleocraft in resin 10,000 years after your death, at 1/35 scale, what would you think? How would you respond to your review in *Prehistoric Times,* no. 41, in the diminutive, as "Meg . . . fat, dumb, and happy"? Is happiness knowing you will be remembered as a monster? What do you know of happiness, or fatness, of the poetry of pain?

Would it please you to know that your model, like yourself, is now out of print, but that, like your bones, traces of it still haunt the expired pages of the Internet? What would it take to know your nut-sized brain, your rudimentary intelligence? What secrets did you know about the world before our own? Would you have advised me not to eat the wild-caught fish or forest mushrooms in Lithuania, irradiated still by Chernobyl, twenty-five years before?

I suspect you knew: to live is to be irradiated. It is a sacrifice, this life. If you got enough, like Godzilla, resurrected lizard, you might be made to feel our rage at being, imagined on the page. Though we never imagined you as arch-foe for the mega-lizard, we might have, offered you up to root against (as we got to know Godzilla, we would often take his side against the other interlopers, because at least he was our terror, and long acquaintance breeds a sympathy), like other pretenders to the throne: Rodan, Megalon, King Kong, Mothra, Ghidorah, Destoroyah, SpaceGodzilla, Hedorah, Mechagodzilla, Gigan, King Caesar, Titanosaurus, Zilla, Orga, Megaguirus, Battra, Gorosaurus, Kumonga, and Minilla.

If given the chance, would you rise and take your place in lights? Would you lay waste to the remains of the Fukushima reactor crossing the Pacific to make land in California in a year, setting America awash in another wave of toxic junk? Or will you arise some day in the future, your displayed bones somehow resurrected after the right sort of disaster, and loose your rage on us?

Knowing that we made you doesn't help the wonder. Even then we were sure that we were right. This is only our most recent mistake; I'm certain it will not be our last.

RHIZOMAL

✓ *The Sound and the Fury* by William Faulkner

✓ *Pope Joan* by Donna Woolfolk Cross

✓ *The Sixteen Pleasures* by Robert Hellenga

✓ *Superstitious* by R. L. Stine

✓ *The Beach* by Alex Garland

✓ *The Man Who Ate Everything* by Jeffrey Steingarten

✓✓ *The Great Gatsby* by F. Scott Fitzgerald

✓ *Memoirs of a Beatnik* by Diane di Prima

✓✓✓✓✓ *High Fidelity* by Nick Hornby

—Reading log, Megan Campbell's personal library (bedside table, top drawer)

How do you read? I am not so orderly as the above: instead, a spaz, a slob, a spiral, I move midway from book to book, stack to stack, thought to thought, labyrinth to labyrinth until I'm headfirst in the thicket. I'm not proud of it, my shallowness, but then a line or reference suggests another, and I ricochet, read, and recollect. Each one illuminates a node and my brain goes *aah* then *more* and opens wider. It will never be enough.

Online I can troll my reading history, every book I have checked out from a library to date, strange paths across the pond—arriving where? Just in the last few years: *Pause and Effect: An Introduction to the History of Punctuation in the West; The Science and Technology of Gelatin;* Gide's *Oedipus and Theseus;* several Michael Ayrton books, a bunch of hoax books and books on hoaxes; the uncollected papers of B. F. Skinner; one of the two Biosphere 2 memoirs; Pessoa; a book on *descansos,* roadside memorials in the Southwest; commonplace books by George Gardner Herrick, Auden, Alec Guinness, and Lovecraft; a couple of books on daylight saving time (in which Arizona does not participate, having enough daylight already, thank you); a book on lawns; two on water crises in the west; Disfarmer's photographs; quite a few Albert Goldbarth books I only just returned; *The Future of Card Catalogs* (from 1975—that ship has since sailed); books on collecting and curating; Scandinavian poets in translation, particularly Inger Christensen; *The Cadaver Dog Handbook;* a lot of Adrienne Rich; *Audio Sweetening for Film and TV; Wireless Telephone and Broadcasting . . .* Only an ellipsis can suggest this list's endlessness. Here's Umberto Eco from his *Infinity of Lists:* "The fear of being unable to say everything seizes us not only when we are faced with an infinity of names but also with an infinity of things." Any reader knows this fear. There's so much here that it's enough to overrun the buffers in the brain and go straight to the sublime. This doesn't even include the ILLs or those books I chose at random from the shelves in my hauntings here and paged through or in some cases read entire and blew an afternoon in another world.

Imagine organizing your shelves in chronological order of your reading life. If you reread a book, you could buy another copy or leave a dummy in its place so as to keep its presence marked. My wife has logged each book she's read since she was young. (The first pages enumerate a lot of V. C. Andrews, which appears to merit no embarrassment: there's no room to be ashamed in a list like this; either she read it or she didn't; nothing gets erased; each check mark indicates another read.) Why'd she read *High Fidelity* six times? How'd she get to Jane Smiley, Norman Rush, then Clive Barker? This list does not explain. Her brother Dave was working his way alphabetically through his library's Fiction—Adult section before he moved out of town. When he left off, he was in the Ds, at Jeffrey Deaver. Can you tell their father is an engineer?

Dear librarian, it must be difficult for you not to want to slip into a favorite patron's reading history. For me the temptation would be great to snoop, to open up our reading lives, these things we might keep even from those we love. What do you make of us?

Think of it, Defacer: if you had checked out the books you marked there would have been a record. Or what of the reader who might have braved the world to check one out and read in private only to have your hatred sprayed across their tenderness? Does our reading life balance or subvert our waking life? So much of us remains submerged until we go diving with or into books. Eco echoes back: "It's not that form cannot suggest infinity. . . . The infinity we are talking about now is an actual infinity made up of objects that can perhaps be numbered but that we cannot number—we fear that their numeration (and enumeration) may never stop."

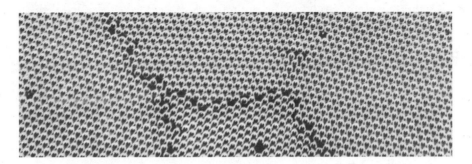

An aggregate of bubbles illustrating the structure of metals on an atomic scale and serving as a visual metaphor for the hierarchy of interactions of all kinds. Note the formation of regions of order that tolerate a few internal local anomalies but conflict on a larger scale to produce linear boundaries of connected disorder.

—Cyril Stanley Smith, *A Search for Structure* (Q171 S618 copy 2, University of Arizona Science & Engineering Library)

Sometimes it just takes a title. Other times an image. A word, a name, a sentence, an idea, then some kind of interaction happens, and you are gone, in memory, synecdoche, one thing standing in for another, the small for the larger. America, for instance. Being gone, you find, is a pleasant presentation of the world: from afar we see these things as lines: roadsprawl, irrigated circles, wires to hold our communications with each other, towers to propagate invisible electricities to our ear, the swaths of forest cut away. The epic simile accomplishes this: a quick zoom out from the micro to the macro, a long Iliadic battle no more than bee frenzy if you step back far enough. All our continental struggles indiscernible when seen from space. A distancing reveals the larger structure. So too magnify enough and we deadhead into structure, and it's not hard on a cold morning with frost on glass to intuit a greater order in loveliness like this.

Why else do we come to books to sentences to words if not to have our heads removed, if not to have those machines press us downward into something gloriously other for a moment, then another, then another. It's barely breathing, thinking of these feelings, articulating them as well as we are able (it's rare that we're so able but the reward of essaying these spaces is enough most days to keep us going from alignment to alignment).

The palm frond, winded, rubbing on the trunk, presents an interruption. The tiny book I carry in which I make notes presents an interruption. The world interrupts thought; thought interrupts world. A girl can do it too: you're there and then no longer, formerly brain, glass eye, reading, hoovering sentences into somewhere else and incomprehensible; now you're a body; there's desire; thoughts of your wife and who she was before, is now, and will be; the soft spots of your life.

I apologize for the interruption in your reading if you found this wedged in this text. Discard it if you like. Leave it out exposed to weather and watch it gust and curl, fade in sun to nothing. That's what these words are worth, long term, just another margin scrawl, another grocery note forgotten here, evidence of a mind grinding on another mind.

I think of Heather here, our house sitter for the month that we were out of the country. A house is a collection. The books there. The objects here. The structures there. The hanging racks of vintage shirts and skirts for use or sale. The formal movements of the pets, hour by hour, as they pursue laps or light or food. The spread of the plants after unexpected rain. What order did she find in our collection?

Perhaps it comes down to faith: why we believe the world cajoles and purls and purrs and grinds you down then suddenly finds an order, a new alignment. *Oh, we say, okay.* Can we model macro with the micro just by quick synecdoche, saying *head of cattle,* just by saying *Megan,* meaning a woman, a history, and world?

Smith replies: "*Everything* involves structural hierarchy, an alternation of external and internal, homogeneity and heterogeneity. Externally perceived quality (property) is dependent on internal structure; *nothing* can be understood without looking not only at it in isolation on its own level but also at both its internal structure and the external relationships which simultaneously establish the larger structure and modify the smaller one. Most human misunderstanding arises less from differing points of view than from perceptions of different levels of significance. The world is a complex system, and our understanding of it comes, in science, from the matching of model structures with the physical structure of matter and, in art, from a perceived relationship between its physical structure and the levels of sensual and imaginative perception that are possible within the structure of our brain's workings."

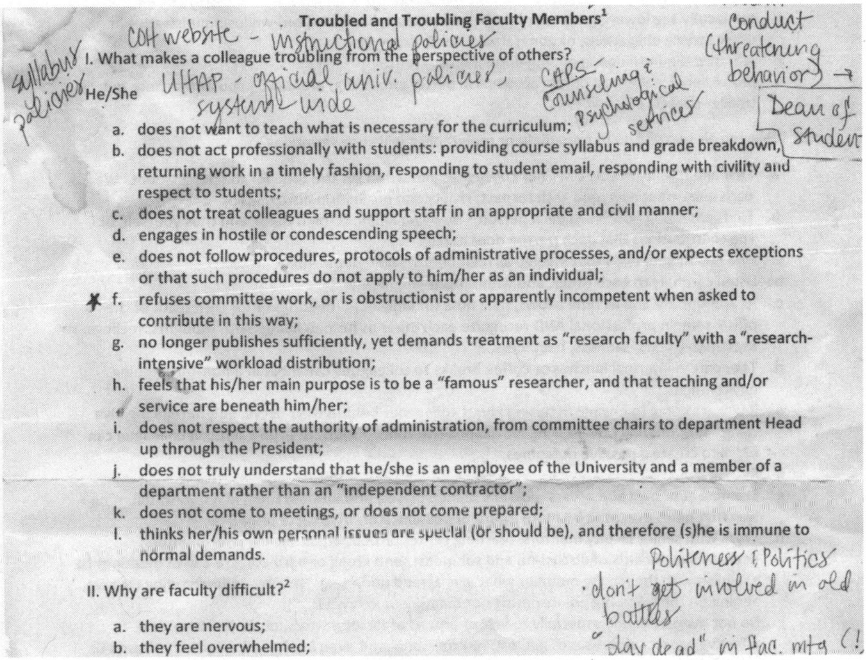

[Handwritten annotations surrounding the reproduced form:] COH website – instructional policies · syllabus policies · UHAP – official univ. policies, system-wide · Counseling & psychological services · CAPS · conduct (threatening behavior) → Dean of Students

Troubled and Troubling Faculty Members[1]

I. What makes a colleague troubling from the perspective of others?

He/She

a. does not want to teach what is necessary for the curriculum;

b. does not act professionally with students: providing course syllabus and grade breakdown, returning work in a timely fashion, responding to student email, responding with civility and respect to students;

c. does not treat colleagues and support staff in an appropriate and civil manner;

d. engages in hostile or condescending speech;

e. does not follow procedures, protocols of administrative processes, and/or expects exceptions or that such procedures do not apply to him/her as an individual;

f. refuses committee work, or is obstructionist or apparently incompetent when asked to contribute in this way;

g. no longer publishes sufficiently, yet demands treatment as "research faculty" with a "research-intensive" workload distribution;

h. feels that his/her main purpose is to be a "famous" researcher, and that teaching and/or service are beneath him/her;

i. does not respect the authority of administration, from committee chairs to department Head up through the President;

j. does not truly understand that he/she is an employee of the University and a member of a department rather than an "independent contractor";

k. does not come to meetings, or does not come prepared;

l. thinks her/his own personal issues are special (or should be), and therefore (s)he is immune to normal demands.

II. Why are faculty difficult?[2]

a. they are nervous;

b. they feel overwhelmed;

[Handwritten annotations:] Politeness & Politics · don't get involved in old battles · "play dead" in fac. mtg (!)

The storm of passion once over, he would have given worlds, had he possessed them, to have restored to her that innocence of which his unbridled lust had deprived her. Of the desires which had urged him to the crime, no trace was left in his bosom. The wealth of India would not have tempted him to a second enjoyment of her person.

—Matthew Lewis, *The Monk* (friends' library)

Don't worry while you're gone, I won't riffle the drawers of lacy negligees or search for porn or evidence of perversion. Instead I'll go straight to your books. How rare, these instances of being in your house without you there, and so I'll take advantage of the silence. Breaking and entering was once a pleasure for this adolescent reason, to know another's life, or its furnishings at least, but this time I have the key. You asked me to feed the cats. So I have fed the cats, cleaned out the mechanical turk of a litterbox you seem to find necessary. Now they are distracted and I can run my hands along your spines, imagine these vertebrae a finger at a time, tip out a couple of titles without losing their place, try to parse the logic of your collection.

Not a library for lending, though I'm sure if I asked, you'd happily let me borrow. And not all yours, I noticed. One of them, your father's, judging from the bookplate: *Towards the Sociology of Knowledge*, edited by Gunter W. Remmling. Another from the university library. Did you forget it here at home? Once I forgot a set of dirty Polaroids in Lawrence Ferlinghetti's *The Coney Island of the Mind*. Was I freer then, I wonder?

Your wife's shelves intrigue me more. Yours overlap well enough with mine, our subjects familiar if not intimate, but hers are often in Italian or translation, thus more exotic, and her marginalia more abundant, frenzied, and explicit. We think of our intellectual lives as a public good here in the academy—how dull that sounds, like tolling bells, the drear of days, echo chambers filled with dust, and such isolation!—but for us the bookshelf is a private space. Marginalia might be plundered by a rival to scoop a dissertation, eviscerate a reputation. What we do is not dramatic until something ruptures, maybe desires take hold of us, and we act, the world breaks, and so do we.

Here Lewis's *The Monk* recounts "the diabolical decline of Ambrosio, a Capuchin superior, who succumbs to temptations offered by a young girl who has entered his monastery disguised as a boy, and continues his descent with increasingly depraved acts of sorcery, murder, incest and torture." Inside I find a memo from the administration on "Troubled and Troubling Faculty Members"—an intended pairing or a happy circumstance? That sort of faculty member "does not act professionally with students," the memo advises, and (you adorned this with a star) "refuses committee work, or is obstructionist or apparently incompetent," as if to elevate these sins together: lust and sloth or maybe spite. What are your sins? What are mine? Our breaking points? Do we share them? Might they share a page in this book, this space, your shelf, your self, both of ours, these hours we carve out to spend with others' words, those netherworlds?

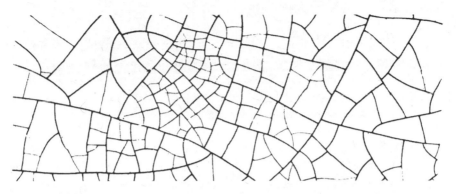

Corrosion is generally regarded as evil, destructive, or at least undesirable. But, like the electrolytic couple that underlies it, corrosion has two sides.

—Cyril Stanley Smith, *A Search for Structure* (Q171 S618 copy 2, University of Arizona Science & Engineering Library)

On the top floor of the Science & Engineering Library there is a whole section still organized by Dewey. An anomaly, since public libraries still mostly use it, but academic libraries switched to the Library of Congress classification system by the latter decades of the twentieth century. This library switched to LC in 1968 and shifted almost all the Dewey volumes in 2008, I find, on asking. But still there are these stacks (016.5 U58 to 697 A493, fourteen aisles, to be exact), orphaned here, still searchable via the online catalog but difficult to find, if one were even looking. A mile away in the Poetry Center library they don't use either LC or Dewey. Instead books are shelved alphabetically (mostly: anthologies are shelved by region) and marked only with accession numbers that numerate their acquisition. They're searchable in the catalog, but that returns no call number.

Any structure will fracture under sufficient pressure. This pressure's budgetary, certainly. But books get written in, lost, marked up, dog-eared, coffee-spilled, food-smeared, torn up, stolen, misclassified, incorrectly reshelved, intentionally misplaced, mutilated, defaced. Books listed in the Dewey section still include *Computer Simulation Techniques* (only doubtfully of use, considering it was published in 1951), *The Theory of Thin Shells*, *Thin Shell Theory*, *The Universe of Space and Time*, *The Ethical Dilemma of Science*, *The Exact Sciences in Antiquity*, and, excellently, Joseph Jastrow's 1936 *The Story of Human Error*. A bit later, at the address 616.8 E58e H.C., find a first printing of O. Spurgeon English and

Gerald H. J. Pearson's 1945 edition of *Emotional Problems of Living*. If a book is a building in which we organize our thoughts, this one's title offers us an open door, a wide one, and I have to pick it up.

On a later page, the following is underlined: "they will eventually tire of each other's company somewhat and will have to live with the rest of the world—and they should be willing and able to do so without jealousy. Marriage is a great test of whether the human being can love someone other than himself; that is, whether he can be considerate of another person." Further on, a heart, a penciled glyph, adorns a section titled "Depression" in the chapter "Reactions to Inevitable Life Situations." When were you last checked out or read, I wonder, and by whom? Dear underlining reader, I wonder at your motivation, what was in your heart when you impressed this heart into the page. Where was your marriage the afternoon you picked up and plowed through this book? What did you want from it—the marriage or the book, or the pairing of the two? Still in the paragraph descending from "Depression," you underlined "mood changes" and "In the psychoneuroses they are extreme." The book's long resided here. The bookplate indicates "Fine Arts Library," "gift of T. E. Hanley." Hanley, was this interloper you or a user of your library? And if I search for human trace in books, what is the limit to what I find?

Hey now, maybe this corrosion of the text isn't just corruption but a feature, meant for a future reader. Its decoration at least indicates its use. Would that we all felt so strongly as to annotate our texts with our intentions, mark the bits that we came looking for and found. Sometimes books are canyons that we enter seeking echoes of our thoughts. In that stricture we can always find a structure and reward ourselves, reminds the intriguing polymath Cyril Stanley Smith: "All things have internal structure. Externally, a thing may have form, and possess considerable grace in the balance of its parts, but it cannot be said to have a style unless some aspect of the relationship of its parts appears in other objects and, by its replication, provides a basis for a perceptive eye to group them together." Do we see ourselves or something else within its sentences?

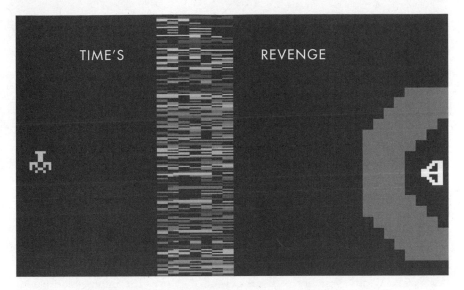

TIME'S   REVENGE

(Learning Games Initiative Research Archive, Tucson, Arizona)

Calling it what it is—a library of games, of video games, primarily, computer games secondarily—evades the clever way it's packaged for the institution. To nestle *games* inside *learning, research,* and *archive* legitimizes our hours in front of screens exploring labyrinths. Maybe it demagnetizes them a little too, peels the pull of illicit play away from the activity at the center: engagement with a text, a puzzle set, a set of rules, a world. More importantly, future lover, isn't this a library of what we thought would be the future? Everything seen on screens, the only printed things the manuals and maps and weird ephemera tucked away inside the cases? Nearly every other text we find encoded in the cartridge, tape, disk, disc, or diskette (how quaint! a little disk! for those of us who care about the difference, which should be all of us who care about information and how we access it, a disk adorned with *k* denotes magnetic media; a disc refers to optical),

An archive is a noble thing: to refer so clearly to the past, to hold the line against erosion, loss, deletion, demagnetization, the work of inattention, there being so much to download or buy and play and delete or give away. Preserving games is difficult. Unlike a (printed) book they require machines to play; operating systems; software subroutines; the proper patches; working paddles, joysticks, or other controllers; the correct cables; and to play those copy-protected games we may need the original media or its packaging. That's a lot to keep, and only heroes care enough to keep it.

Of course the LGI is buried in a building far from the quad, where few would stumble on it unless directed. On the top floor of the Transitional Office Building, named for the act of dislocation, the hope of aspiration to a better space, open the door and find wonders beyond your wildest whatever. This is why I love a university: like an Advent calendar, each door reveals a treasure. A huge TV connects to half a dozen game systems behind a few PCs; to the right, display cases covered over with felt where the really weird is kept. On the left, a wall of desiccated snacks.

Then there's the door that takes you into the shelves. On the shelves there are the games: cartridges, tapes, CDs, disks and discs. It flatlines the mind and takes you back in time: where was this when you were fourteen? You could spend a year in here or more. All the major gaming consoles of your lifetime and most of the minor ones: Atari Jaguar, the Neo Geo, Vectrex Arcade System, Wonder Wizard Sharp Shooter, SG-1000 II, the Sega Nomad, the Odyssey 300, TI-99/4A, Astrocade Arcade, varieties of Atari beyond memory. The impossible-to-find, offensive games for the Atari: *Custer's Revenge* or *Beat'Em and Eat'Em*, pornographic titles that barely earn the name *game*. Needless to say that you could jawdrop here and never pick it up and play yourself or the world to death.

This is a library of selves inasmuch as it is a library of games. Here you can access again who you were when you lost yourself in a summer of *Alien vs. Predator* on the Jaguar wasted and glorious with your friends. Or the year when your mother died and a cousin came to play endless games of *Missile Command* and *Space Invaders* with you, those nights when adults were downstairs working their way through sadness. You were working too. You're still working. Maybe sadness is a game, a maze, a labyrinth in which you're made to reel but still you feel you're circling to a central point. Emotion is a motion, action, process, and a destination. Of course you found your way there too. A game could delay but not defeat it. In retrospect perhaps this is the moment that cemented games' hold on/role in your emotional life.

Even if it there was no meaning in *Breakout!*'s bricks in glowing walls removed with pixelated balls, what you felt before you turned to the screen found its way there too. You were breaking something down to see what was behind it. Or in *Yars' Revenge*, you chipped away the wall around a glowing, strobing thing (was it a heart?), only to lance it—when revealed—with a cannon.

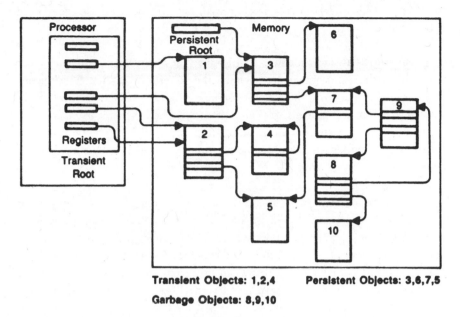

Transient Objects: 1,2,4   **Persistent Objects: 3,6,7,5**

Garbage Objects: 8,9,10

Figure 2. Uniform Memory Abstraction

—Stanley B. Zdonik and David Maier, eds., *Readings in Object-Oriented Database Systems* (QA 76.9 D3 R42 1990)

There are twelve objects in this memory. Three are transient, four persistent, and four are garbage: but which is which, you wonder: The orange bowl? The oranges in the bowl as they crest the top. The peeled shrimp you ate all of. The blue bowl that held the shrimp you stuffed your face with. A drive-thru fast-food restaurant on the Florida coast that served your order in pneumatic tubes. A jellyfish, or its corpse. A purple dress. Your father's hand. Your brother's hair. A rock. A cloud of blocky, pixelated tsetse flies from the Atari 2600 game *Raiders of the Lost Ark*.

They are connected but you don't know how except they're yours for now, sieved out of the brainwash. Why they're not flushed is hard to say. These things are flushed from time to tide, or you think they are, and few are left, then they are reconfigured. Some stay the same. Our brains are all abstractions, loops, one abstraction chained to another for no apparent reason. There has to be a reason. We like to think we are made of reason, alone among the animals, to be able to make sense out of what's collected in the box. Given ten random inputs, the brain will storyboard, concoct a narrative, what happened on the drive to the drive-in where your parents took you to a double feature: *Alien* and a porno, as you remember. It goes without saying, as you remember. What else is there but memory? They wouldn't admit it even if you asked, even if you could ask them, even if they could answer.

There the film is always showing. Though it's black and white, you're sure the bowl is blue. That one's orange, it's obvious. The actress's lips, a double-curve on-screen, suggest your own, the flick of tongue a ping: the taste of shrimp, fresh, briny in a bowl, then the memory of gluttony, then a bell and salivation, and now you want to masturbate. Fuck this brain, you think, its big top circuit circus. There's something here to discover—something spotlit, if you can only remember or sift some sense from it.

You were three, or so your parents said. You should have no memories of that time but yet you do, and they're not of your mother—who's dead, you always have to say—but of these pointless sparks. Throw them in the sky: a constellation. Chart them on a pie. Scatter-plot and best-fit-line them by etymology, alphabetical order, frequency in American literary fiction 1945 to 1975, the year that you were born, that year must mean something, too, that it was the year British artist and dweller/maker of labyrinths Michael Ayrton died, and you'd discover him thirty-four years later in a tiny library in Florida, not far from the site of this memory, amidst the prehistoric plants that twine seamlessly underneath everything growing or not. Those plants—that network of root and spur—those electricities—and the insects that use them as catwalks to other worlds, they must mean something too, if only you were smart enough to see it or know that you were seeing something temporary, before the figures reconfigure in the box and, Rorschach, start to resolve into a different thing, before your brain moves on to narrative one thousand three hundred thirty-four of the day: the artist just short of reaching transcendental state and seeing something as it truly is, you know, like in myth, but instead resolving back to sleep, another shuffling of the deck.

> I was hooked by the words on the page and by the page itself,
> pliable and tough, stained, deep in the paper's weave, with
> flecks of dark color. The binding was limber. I was breathing

. . . quickly. I'd been curious to see the Folger's books, yet had not anticipated their durability and powerful tactile appeal. They'd existed for such a long time. As my guide and I rode the elevator back up to the main reading room, I wondered who I might call on the phone. To whom could I blurt out the excitement of peering into these books? As I remember, I called my father, who listened patiently while I described the sensation of holding the *Arcadia* and the *Shepherd's Calendar* and *A Midsummer Night's Dream*. What I am getting at is the idea that books do not in all cases merely *convey* the content on their pages; in some fundamental respect, books, especially the most beautiful, shelter and accommodate their contents.

—Donald Antrim, *The Afterlife* (PS3551.N85 Z46 2006)

You get at least two afterlives. One resides in memory, not yours, but another's. You don't get to choose whose. The other is in the disposition and dispersion of your books. In what order they were read, how quickly, what for, what notes you left, the naked Polaroids you hid between their pages, which titles you gave or lent, to whom, and why (to woo? to educate? to correct? to offer an alternative? to improve another's heart?), and how well that went over (let me guess: it was not a hit).

I have no books from my father's library. None from my mother either that I remember. He is still alive, so it is not too late. Did he ever give me one? I remember a couple arrived one year from Amazon as a gift, in the modern way. Last month he left *Ghost Soldiers* by Hampton Sides in our guest room, so perhaps that counts. On page 62 the word *fucked* is crossed out in "All those fate-fucked men whose boats left just before theirs were supposed to, who sailed on to this American colony halfway around the world to be sacrificed like goats." Later, in chapter 12, there are a lot of words underlined, another *fuck* crossed out and one *goddam*. That is the extent of the redactions and significations.

I expect these are not my father's marks. He's not the sort to cross out words, mark up his books, or keep them around for longer than he'd need to blow through them in a weekend visit. (Or perhaps he is, and I've discovered, not too late, an important fact.)

Sometimes Edgar Allan Poe pursued a hypnagogic state to open up a seam into the world. Through this came these "fancies," as he called them, "not thoughts . . . shadows of shadows . . . seem to me rather psychal than intellectual. . . . I am aware of [them] only when I am upon the very brink of sleep, with the consciousness that I am so. . . . This condition exists but for an inappreciable point of time" (from his collected marginalia, containing, among other things, his riffing on the usefulness of margins as a place for self-communication if not notes to others—in this way I read these notes as notes to me a future later).

Some nights I achieve the same without trying, slip into the haze without intention. I don't believe in the transcendence of the gloaming space between the waking life and the one we spend asleep, sentenced to walk labyrinths at the mercies of our books. I don't know that we can touch the other by working in the spaces just past waking. But I'll admit I can see a glimmer in the margin, peripheral vision: surely it's not all whiteness, vacuum, empty space, an accident of typography. Sometimes the page appears porous as gauze, and I see through to an emanation from the other side, even if, upon inspection, it's just a printer's faulty registration on the verso page. That too has a voice. It moves its mouth. It's trying to find its way to speech.

I mean to say that in these self-transcriptions we leave ourselves and we find ourselves again, a decade later, say, or check back in a generation, see what our children have made of our fucked penmanship (don't you know that the ways of cursive, like the children, were once our certain future?) or the moments you saw fit to argue with the text or compose asides. *Fuck* was important enough to our forebears, they will say, to scrawl out with pen. This is assuming anyone reads, of course, and that we have not wiped the planet clean and written over it with zeroes so deep the next reader could not possibly unerase our data spools and understand our need to believe in something after all of this even in the face of all evidence to the contrary.

... until it melts beneath your heart ... until you can't bear it any longer. Pain stays there forever until you talk about pain. It washes away and never comes back until sorrow. By Zevi Shane Bloomfield

—Handwritten sympathy card, Tucson Public Library, Eckstrom-Columbus Branch (filed under *Collective memory--United States; Bereavement; Death--Social aspects; Mourning customs--United States; Memorialization; Memory; Giffords, Gabrielle D. [Gabrielle Dee], 1970--Assasination* [sic] *attempt, 2011; Condolence notes; Tucson [Ariz.]*)

Can a library collect or catalog pain? Some try. Often memorials by name (this one's named for Dan Eckstrom, who is still alive), many hold a sorrow story, someone lost to past and now just the branch's name.

Today I came here for the gallery. The January 8 exhibit features sympathy notes, cards, and posters from the 2011 shooting of my congresswoman, Gabrielle Giffords, and many others at a Safeway not far away. After the blood faded and the temporary memorial material was collected at the hospital, the Arizona Memory Project archived and cataloged what notes and cards and signs they could. Today they are displayed: not the pain itself but the evidentiary bruise, each note an outline of the strike, a wet echo spreading, gas expanding from an extinguished star. From the fragment we intuit what was here before.

Mostly these are notes from kids. It's hard not to be moved. Many are addressed to Christina-Taylor Green, 9/11/01–1/8/11; she too was killed on that day three years ago. Since then her life would have expanded by a third.

We are made up of mostly water, as they say. Most libraries archive words, our better parts, but one library holds only water: Iceland's Library of Water offers twenty-four volumes, each a melt, an archive of a separate glacier or its future state. There too find silence and a sense of dwindling—or perhaps renewing. You may pass through but borrow only in the sense of memory. We might think: all water is for lending; all we do is hold it for a while, then release. Bloomfield tells us pain is water but that it will not wash away. At best by talk it can be transmuted into sorrow. An archive is a kind of talk, waiting for an answer.

Unrelated, I presume, a sign on a meeting room advertises WIDOW WIDOWER MEETING happening right now. Widow, meet widower. Widower, meet widow. Let's look at the window together and remember there is something beyond this room. Here we're all wrecked; we're all wet; here we're all lonely, learning again how to live. We know we must forget to progress or move past but we don't know what, how much, how often—how to let go of anything at all. How do we release? When does it cease?

January 8, 2014

If, as was axiomatic in romantic theory, the potter left his thumbprints on the vase, then a knowledge of his life, his personality, and the conditions of the age that affected them could help define the special qualities of the works to which his name was attached.

—Richard D. Altick, *Lives and Letters: A History of Literary Biography in England and America,* 1966 (unmarked library, English and Counseling Services 021, Kansas State University)

Because the glass was broken on the case I let myself inside. Left alone these books might waste away unread, I reasoned, and any book good enough to be locked away must be worth a read. Inside I found the *Collected Poems of Edwin Arlington Robinson,* seventeenth printing. Is it surprising that I never heard of him? I haven't always read well or deeply, at times at all. Yet I have loved books. I just pulled a collection off my shelf, where it's been filed, unread, since 2008, when I received a copy from the University of Michigan Press with a note from their publicist. Seems I had asked for a review copy, even if I never read the note or book enclosed until I opened it today and read an essay, then consigned it to Goodwill. My apologies to Stephanie the publicist. You can't hold on to everything.

I'm not so good at social things. I know codices are social too, but in them we play a longer game. The connection time for books isn't measured in hours or days: a decade is not so much. Robinson's *Collected* was published in 1965. Sometimes you need to grow into a book, or steal and haul it across the country only to discard it, or just happen on it in a collection. They're durable that way. Unlike the modem's handshaking shushing garbled sound that used to play when we connected our machines to another's, a little sex-spark in the Michigan night, they don't give away their secrets so easily.

What consolation, then, to be here in the little apple of Manhattan (Kansas), perusing your unmarked and donated library, W. R. Moses, poet and teacher at Kansas State who died a decade ago. I didn't know your poems either until now. There is still so much to be read. I found two copies here of your *Collected Poems,* too, so I liberated one. (Again with this delinquency? I know, I know, but won't apologize. Turnabout's just fine: reader, please feel free to take a card, a page, or this book entire: your theft will honor me.)

Inside this copy of Robinson's *Collected* I find a torn bookflap and a receipt dated 5 July 1968 from "Rich's, a Southern Institution Since 1867." Until 2005 Rich's was a beloved Atlanta department store, bought out and plowed under by Macy's. Here too, a handwritten note: "Merlin has been in timeless wisdom, but is drawn to Vivian, into time, to grief. . . . Lancelot . . . would at last have forsaken the light for [Guinevere], but she refused, and he rode into darkness/light (and death, apparently)." From your signature on your MA student Bernadette Krassoi's 1978 thesis, "Edwin Arlington Robinson: The Torch of Woman," I can see this is your hand.

Orhan Pamuk tells me that "museums—just like novels—can also speak for individuals." Sure, a library's no museum, nor mausoleum, even if you're dead, but I think the principle's the same, that through books and notes and artifacts we can (to some extent) understand and reconstruct the librarian's brain.

To that end I go back further. In a February 1946 issue of *Poetry* you write, "Crumpled, disappointing substitute / For any kind of letter from anyone at all, / Here's nothing in the mailbox" ("Sentimental Reflection"). Dear W. R. Moses, I can't know what you thought of the future, how it might remember or contain you like a cocoon. But, half-assed as I am, I am your future reader—and I am your future lover—and if I could I would send a letter back through time to you.

i was thinking about this while i was flying toward iowa and thinking about
how everyone was going to be trying to locate the avant-garde   / and about
how almost everyone was going to agree that it would involve either shock-
ing or making it new   / and i was supposed to be talking about this too   /
and i realized i was going to be confused   / because practically every role
classically attributed to the avant-garde has been preempted by something
else   / and i reflected that i myself have never really had a clear image of
what it was to be avant-garde   / though ive been thrust into the role often
enough to know what it feels like to be avant-garde   / . . . and i tried to consider the nature of the fit   / between the life we lead and the death we get

—David Antin, *what it means to be avant-garde*, 1993
(University of Arizona Poetry Center Library)

Oh anxious and ambitious heart, who is ever good enough for the avant-garde?
You try to hold your edge, to look mean or at least serious, to wear your monocle
without laughing, watch trains at the crossing, worry your carbuncle until it
starts to drain. Not you, surely; not a row of *you*s lined up like trees along a lane
and butchered into matches by tornado wind, scattered onto walls and called art.
We might as well call them *orts*, offal, assorted scraps, essay chunks remaindered
from whatever argument you thought you were making at the time. A decade
has a way of humbling you. That's what they're for, decades, arcades in which
you sucked at *Bubble Bobble*, dodecahedrons you once tossed in daylong games
of *D&D*, failing at originality in your plot contrivances, your eating powdered
sugar by the bag, your eroding teeth.

Oh self-deprecating heart, try the library shelves filled with those who meant to
ride the leading edge of art filed away with equally ambitious others. Rack their
corpses—all that breath, all those manifestos—up in stacks, spine to spine, each
cutting a swath through the one before. Their edge too has passed and now paves
the center of the path. They are now as gaseous clouds, remaindered, filtered into
books. If to be avant-garde is to oppose the center, what happens when the center spreads and brings you in like a little bear? So what if your methods are ad-
opted slash co-opted? If we find ourselves surrounded, what is there to do but
cut ourselves apart, offer our hearts up in snippet bits, 140 characters at a time, to
feed the younger, harder, hotter? It does not speak so well of you, your life, your
tiny history of strife, your desire for more for new for you forever.

Oh Bruce Springsteen–quoting heart, you are—you stay—so hungry. It's okay. You could eat at Olde Country Buffet every day for a decade and still not reach a state of satiation. Hunger fuels the go, that open-mouthed Pac-Man approach to the world, that restlessness, that resistance to the rubbing motion you're feeling: it's just erosion, friction, function of the fast. Ignore the cool: find the real. Bruce Mau tells us "cool is conservative fear dressed in black." Instead, explore the fear.

Oh timid heart, why do you ask to justify your ways? The history of the avant-garde is the history of art. Isn't that enough? Only in experiment is anything achieved. But experiment can't be where it ends up. To what end, this experiment? What good is this new form? Is this the best way or just a new way? What spaces have you uncovered in your exploration? What are you writing around? How does it make you feel or think on reading, on writing? What terror are you protecting? How far will you go? And why? And when?

Oh bell-dumb heart, it makes you a fool to think you were ever closer to opening up the world—to art, to breaking it apart—than those who came before. But knowing that can't make you read or breathe more slowly. Since when did you listen to anyone? To give up on innovation is to give up on the work we do with alphabet and light. It's not enough to hunt or haunt our parents' hearts; we must occupy our own.

As we look back have we any ground at all for a feeling of superiority about our present-day theory? . . . What of the future? Since in all our theories we use concepts (such as fields) which of their nature cannot be said to be absolutely true or false (*Essays in Electronics* (Iliffe, Chap. 1) there may come a day when it will be found more convenient to use some alternative concepts.

—Cathode Ray [M. G. Scroggie], "Basic Theory Since 1911,"
Wireless World, April 1971 (TK 5700 W55, University of Arizona
Science & Engineering Library)

In the underground of Science & Engineering, among the whole run of periodicals like *Wireless World* and *Bell System Technical Journal* (in which things like the best strategies for communicating holograms are essayed and diagrammed), I hear the sound of furious typing, clackety as on a PC keyboard, and I am impressed by the industriousness of the corresponding graduate student corralled in the carrel. Early morning, late May, and the sun has duly driven the city indoors, into our air-conditioned basement hearts, where we take apart machines.

Investigating closer, the sound becomes inhuman, no typist but a rattling baffle in the air duct. In this way a thing becomes another in a second, the airflow shifts, dust from the stairway drywaller enveloping everything, or perhaps it's just in my nose and breath and the world is hereby filtered through its scent: the world gone dry, gone wall, gone flat, gone dust.

This is the problem with the future, how to use what we think we know right now to lever open an idea into understanding, knowing all the while that this is not knowledge but a best fit line among the scatter plot in view of what we think we know, and not much of one, at that.

I don't think it's just that what survives of us is love, quoting Larkin's "An Arundel Tomb," but our best guesses about what we thought we understood, how we made a nest of thought and chewed up wood and paper pulp and misheard typing sound, and cogitated, lonely little clouds, in corners of the air-conditioned indoor world, how we thought we had something to say about the void, and said it as loudly as we could into the void, as that void, voiceless, ceaseless, muttered absolutely nothing back.

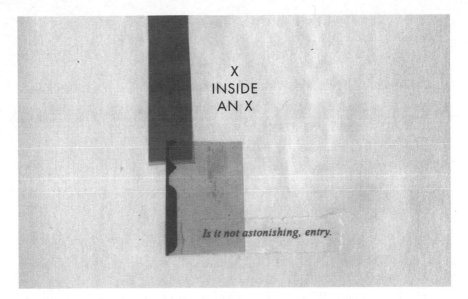

X
INSIDE
AN X

Is it not astonishing, entry.

—Anne Carson, *Nox*

Dear reader of this *Nox*, this book cradled in a box, approximation of an epitaph for Carson's brother, an accordion-folded text, a series of collaged scraps, photographs, correspondence bits, and glosses of translation. Barely typeset, its apparent undesignedness brings us physical intimacy: reading we're aware of Carson's hands, even if it's an artifice, as they pressed snippet *x* into place with staple or with glue. That is, you're aware of Anne, you're interfacing Anne.

Canada is cold and filled with distance. I think of another Canadian, Margaret Atwood, and her invention the LongPen, which allows the writer to sign her books remotely for a reader, to meet her via real-time video in a bookstore, to mime a pen nib pressed into the title page and have the apparatus make the movements in your stead a thousand miles away with ink, so as to mediate a momentary intimacy with technology and grace the page with human sigil.

A book should be graced with human sigil. *Nox* is filled with it, her brother's bits, collected, though none of Anne's handwriting is in evidence. Reading *Nox* at night, there's snow outside like Canada, a tableau of white surprise because we are here, Anne's ghost hand, her dead brother, and I, in Tucson, Arizona, well away from frozen home and my own brother (whether he is cold, whether he sees snow, whether he is alive, I cannot know). A flake lands on the ledge, is cold, considers holding form a moment, disappears.

What else disappears: your time, your drink, your consciousness: consider rate—distance over time—when reading *Nox*. This is what we hope for, to lose ourselves in stream and look up some hours later and note that the world has moved: the cat's crept closer, following the sun. We often move through books more quickly than is wise. Slow, and reading reminds us of what we mark with the action of a turning page: an index finger's synecdoche. The slight lopsidedness of the box is physical, its verso opening slightly larger than the recto, so as to nest when closed. Reading in the box, the accumulating stack pulls slightly down. A spread hangs, inflates a little, a body under a bedsheet, just enough to suggest fullness. Is this awkward effect intentional? Is a question a question or just an opening for your consideration? Is it us opening and considering our opening, considering our opining?

Reading's an opening, a translation, imperfect fit of cloud of mind that disappears into or behind a word when we inscribe it: we might write *here* and mean any *here* at all: your *here* (and you're here now hearing this line resound—my awkward Rs that melt into Ws or Ls when I get lazy—in this I am for a moment resurrected in your mouth or in the axis of your inner ear) or mine or Anne's or any in between. This is not even considering the distances between us. In some mythologies we need intermediaries to speak to the dead. In some mythologies we believe in books to guide our wanderings and those of the recently released.

A pause: night now and away from book, I'm playing Scrabble rip-off *Words with Friends* on my smartphone with my thumb. I am cherishing the *x*. Prototypical algebraic variable, collision of two consonants, internal pluralized (two Ecks combined, perhaps Johann Maier von Eck, who tried to fuse the beliefs of Martin Luther and Jan Hus, and his brother, back to back), it always spots the mark, dots the pox, chants the hex, suggests the sex. I hold on to it longer than I should. I disconnect myself from the post office waiting line and here exist instead as server light and information. Asynchronicity is what makes it work, that you can reach across (a crux is a crucifix only if it's affixed with body, blood, or the simulation of one or both; once a crucifix it cannot again become a cross, even if disassembled, even if the body has been excised. If plastic it may be disposed. If blessed [and therefore sacramental], it should be returned to the earthly elements—water, earth, fire, or air; usually one chooses fire because it works the fastest, is the sexiest. If sacred it must be preserved entire or one sins) a state time zone a country the work of weeks and silences between friends (a less engaging game) to interface in this small way.

Books are intermediaries—asynchronous and slow. A box like this is where it all collects, if you let it, the leftovers of a person (as in a meal shared but not completed and then brought home and perhaps abandoned), what their index fingers touched and left behind, how they wrote what bits they wrote, how they crossed their Ts, how they wore their shirts, how they slashed their exes through and cut them out of their lives. Reading *Nox* is reckoning with the dead: her dead and your own, your death and mine. Or: read backward, a text like this reflowers phoenix-like, is not extinguished. Read backward, your life, your brother's life, is less a tragedy; we might find meaning in its apogee and eventual descent.

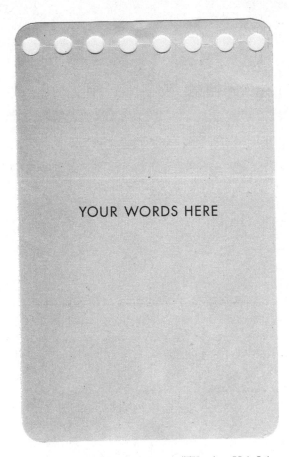

YOUR WORDS HERE

—Mary Ellis Ames, *Balanced Recipes* (TX17.A54, Hale Library
Special Collections, Kansas State University)

Are you getting the idea I must like theft? It's true I stole this page from special collections. If I held the library sacrosanct, I wouldn't touch it, use it, brush my hands along a page, slowly eroding or decomposing it. To use a book is to destroy it. It's okay to treat technology this way. This is what makes it precious, worthy of collection. I choose instead to see a library as a vessel, tool, a place for fools to query reference librarians with their lazy questions that they could have Googled, yes, but more than that, an opportunity for avatar, home for budding atavists just rediscovering the smell and feel of books: so old school sensory, like the Boston Medical Dispensary, which "afforded the means of relief to many necessitous persons, among others, whose feelings would have been hurt by an application for assistance from the alms house."

This page itself doesn't have much smell. *Balanced Recipes,* not quite the first Pillsbury cookbook, but an early one, published in 1933, sold to Pillsbury customers for $1.25, bound in an aluminum shell, so as to protect it from the elements of cookery in the kitchen, includes a set of extra sheets, for the reader's recipes or notes. Ring-bound, it was meant for use, not preservation. Still, Kansas State University library has preserved it, where it lodges in their special collections, which specializes (awesomely) in cookbooks, KSU being the ag and land-grant school of Kansas. The librarian was pleased to show me some of the weirdest items in their collection: '90s rapper Coolio's 2009 cookbook, *Cookin' with Coolio* (his YouTube series deserves your click and awe: dude can cook, is amusing), this lovely metal-bound piece of history, and a stranger recent text, *Cooking with Cum* (pause here for your *ew*). Indecorous to write about or think about, still it's an entry in the category, and thus deserving of collection. Animal product that it is, why should it provoke the cringe response when paired with cooking? Is it because it comes from us?

Yes, I stole a sheet from now-dead-as-of-1968 Mary Ellis Ames; don't think less of me. If you do, at least do it with panache. If you're a librarian of a certain stripe, I'm sure your eyebrow's raised already. But the sheets are blank. They're here for you—for me—for us. I just partook of what was offered. To do less would be to disrespect the book. If I could reinsert this text I would (as you know I publish these back into the books when possible). As long as pages remain you get the point: this book was meant for your hands, handiwork, handwriting, hand-wringing over how much butter, lard, or whatever other animal product is wise, okay, too gross for words, or best to cook with or eat, according to whatever study's just published on the subject: it asks you to engage. It's open-source and open-binding. It wants you to buy more Pillsbury's Best Flour and bake with it, marvel at it, mean it.

Ames was director of Pillsbury's Cooking Service, and she existed. She wrote this book. She left these blank pages in the back for you. She was no faux, no crock, no fabricated brand like Betty Crocker, who was developed by the Washburn Crosby Company in 1921 as a more intimate signatory to respond to baking questions. Fake heart, Crocker's signature was that of a company secretary who won a contest. Played by thirteen different radio actresses, she was given a portrait in 1936, a composite of four different women. An avatar, a shell, having no life proper, she still lives and gives advice; since then her portrait has changed seven times—strange, these worlds inside names.

Suddenly we find ourselves at Z. Like walking out along a pier in fog, an apparent infinity finds its end and we act surprised, as if infinities exist, as if we believed there was nothing more than this. In the Poetry Center's library, which is simply alphabetical, those named with Zs occupy the ends of stacks until they are discarded and freed from tyranny. It would take a lifetime to reach them if you were reading alphabetically like my brother-in-law, unless you lacked charity and closed books after a page.

In the Library of Congress system Z is mostly meta, containing Bibliography, Library Science, and Information Resources (General), which falls under ZA, the only current category that follows it. Peer at Z long enough and you'll uncover: paleography, "Cryptography, Ciphers. Invisible Writing," "Typewriters. Typewriting. Keyboards. Keyboarding," book design, printers' marks, incunabula, classes of libraries, automation, library personnel, "Alphabetizing. Filing," library history and theory, "Anonyms and Pseudonyms," "Thefts and Losses of Books and Other Library Materials," and private libraries. ZA jumps from books into other media, including sound recordings, the embarrassingly dated "Information Superhighway," eventually terminating in Government Information. Oddly the LC classification system has no entries at this time under I, O, W, X, or Y. I and O get skipped probably because of confusion with the digits 1 and 0, and I presume the other letters are left open for inevitable expansion.

There are other ways to classify and shelve, of course, most obviously Dewey, used by 80 percent of libraries, but there's also Harvard-Yenching (obscure, for Chinese language materials, but still used by some), Brinkler (which is more patron-focused and sports a geographical approach), Universal Decimal Classification, Colon Classification (primarily in India), BISAC, VLIB 1.2, folksonomy (crowdsourcing classifications via tagging [and we duly note that its self-study category is, gloriously, *folksontology*]). Then there are the highly specialized, including NLM (for medicine), Dickinson (for music), a handful of Asian systems for those who eschew the Roman alphabet, and Sveriges Allmänna Biblioteksförening (Sweden). The list continues, and far more have gone defunct.

Here I think of Jan Kempenaers's *Spomenik,* widescreen photographs of Spomeniks—huge, abstract, geometric sculptures in the former Yugoslavia, installed in the 1960s and 1970s. As the accompanying narrative explains, "Every single one of them is a memorial monument to the most atrocious events of the Second World War, marking the sites of bloody battles and concentration camps." Most were demolished or vandalized in the 1990s. He photographed a couple dozen of those remaining and presents them without interpretation, translation, or reference. From this vantage point they're unreadable, alien, roughly in the *Barbarella* style. Because of the complicated politics, "the war monuments could assume neither a heroic nor a patriotic guise. In other words, they had to be neutral enough to be acceptable to both victims and perpetrators," and so they remain, inscrutable, increasingly overgrown, and silent all throughout the countryside.

Fast-forward a thousand years. Will our remaining monuments be these systems, these partly arbitrary orders, these ways to code our information? Let's not forget these too are political. Critics of Dewey note that its religion section over represents Christianity: "spanning 220 (Bible) to 289 (Other denominations & sects). Other faiths, such as Judaism (296), get just one division, while Islam is lumped with Babism and Bahai Faith at 297," according to an article in the *Wall Street Journal* about the controversy over a new public library in Gilbert, Arizona, eschewing Dewey.

Everything we've written, what we've read, what we've collected, what we've bookmarked on what pages, what notes we left pressed herein, what we have included, discarded, defaced, lost and then replaced, how it's filed and organized: it's all a carrier, a vector, an edifice of us.

ACKNOWLEDGMENTS

When possible, each of these essays was originally published (on a 6" x 9" card) back into the space (typically the book or library) that started it. The limited edition of this book collected them, unbound and unordered, in a box. Though they are bound here, no meaning is intended by their ordering. They are simply ordered alphabetically.

Since their original publications (as cards), some of these essays have subsequently appeared in magazines, anthologies, or elsewhere, as follows:

Country Music Death Notices — *Dazed & Confused*
Crime of Omission — *Spolia*
Dear Alison, Dear Albert — *Covered with Fur*
Dear Bound — *Quarter After Eight*
Dear Defacer 1, 2, 3, 4, 5 — *A Public Space*
Dear Defacer [Like Emily] — *Flaunt*
Dear Errata — *Black Warrior Review*
Dear Future Lover — *Ecotone*
Dear Futurist Lover — *Mississippi Review*
Dear Sepulcher (Dear Bless Your Heart) — *The Dictionary Project*
Dear Silence Lover — *Mississippi Review*
Dear Squash — *Orion*
Dear Tom Chiarella — *Wag's Revue*
Dear Unsighted — *West Branch Wired*
Disambiguation — *Los Angeles Review*
The Erotic Ocean — *Flaunt*
Everything's Rings, Everything's Signed, For an Odd Geographer — Denis
    Wood, *Everything Sings*, 2nd ed. (Siglio Press, 2013)
The Fold — *Menagerie*
Hide and Seek — *Columbia*
Holding Pattern — *Airplane Reading*
How to Read a Book [Oh, snap] — *Triquarterly*
In Hennepin — *Bending Genre* blog
In Recording Your Attendance — *Mississippi Review*
Introduction to [Biological] Membranes — *Indiana Review*
July Letter — *West Branch*
Know Your Lake Effect — *Hick Poetics*, ed. Abraham Smith and Shelly Taylor
    (Lost Roads Press, 2015)
Letter to a Future Highlighter — *Spolia*

◊

SOME NOTES

"Letter to a Future Lover [Handwritten]" is for Megan
"In Hennepin" is for Jon and Clint
"Questions for Megatherium" is after a line by Paul Guest
"See You Next Week" is for Paul and Aileen
"Transient and Persistent Memory Objects" is for Leonard

◊

THANKS TO

The Arizona Commission on the Arts; Wendy Burk; Elizabeth Dodd; Katie Dublinski; Aileen Feng; Cliff Hight, Morse Department of Special Collections, Kansas State University Library; Lisa Hodgkins, Peggy J. Schlusser Memorial Philatelic Library; the Howard Foundation; Paul Hurh; Barbara Jordan, Tuscaloosa Public Library; Ken McAllister, Learning Games Initiative; Dinty W. Moore; Steve Orlen; Lisa Pearson; Aurelie Sheehan; Jeff Shotts; Hayri Yildirim, University of Arizona Libraries.

This book was written with the partial support of an Artist Research and Development Grant from the Arizona Commission on the Arts and a Howard Foundation Fellowship from Brown University.

This book was also printed in a limited edition, unbound and unordered in a deluxe box.

Ander Monson edits the magazine *DIAGRAM* and the New Michigan Press. He is the author of *Vanishing Point: Not a Memoir,* which was a finalist for the National Book Critics Circle Award in criticism; *The Available World; Neck Deep and Other Predicaments; Other Electricities;* and *Vacationland.* He lives in Tucson and teaches at the University of Arizona.

More: www.otherelectricities.com

The text of *Letter to a Future Lover* is set in Adobe Caslon Pro. Book design by Rachel Holscher. Composition by Bookmobile Design & Digital Publisher Services, Minneapolis, Minnesota. Manufactured by Friesens on acid-free, 100 percent postconsumer wastepaper.